THE ARAB CONQUESTS
OF THE MIDDLE EAST

BRENDAN JANUARY

TWENTY-FIRST CENTURY BOOKS
MINNEAPOLIS

Consultant: Josh Messner, Islamic Studies Program, Luther Seminary, Saint Paul, Minnesota

Primary source material in this text is printed over an antique-paper texture.

Front cover: *The image on the jacket and cover is a miniature from a thirteenth-century copy of the eleventh-century* Scylitzes Chronicle. *It depicts a battle that took place in A.D. 842 between the Byzantines and Arabs.*

Twenty-First Century Books
A division of Lerner Publishing Group, Inc.
241 First Avenue North
Minneapolis, MN 55401 U.S.A.

Website address: www.lernerbooks.com

Library of Congress Cataloging-in-Publication Data

January, Brendan.
    The Arab conquests of the Middle East / by Brendan January.
        p.   cm. — (Pivotal moments in history)
    Includes bibliographical references and index.
        ISBN 978–0–8225–8744–6 (lib. bdg. : alk. paper)
        1. Islamic Empire—History—622–661—Juvenile literature. I. Title.
    DS38.1J355 2009
    956'.013—dc22   2008027022

Manufactured in the United States of America
1 2 3 4 5 6 – BP – 14 13 12 11 10 09

CONTENTS

CHAPTER ONE
"RECITE!"

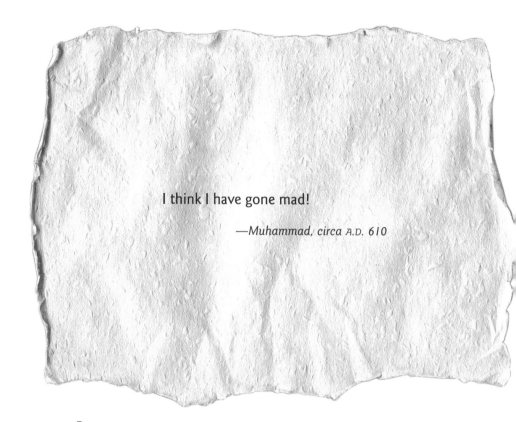

I think I have gone mad!

—*Muhammad, circa* A.D. *610*

It began in a lone cave. In the early A.D. 600s, a prosperous merchant named Muhammad sought out solitude in the hills near his city. The city, Mecca, is on the Arabian Peninsula— the homeland of the Arab people. Muhammad spent hours in the silence of a cave on Mount Hira, meditating and reflecting.

During one of these sessions, something strange happened. Muhammad gasped as an immense pressure

Modern-day pilgrims visit the Prophet's Cave on Mount Hira, near the city of Mecca, Saudi Arabia. This cave is said to be the place where Muhammad first heard the call to become a prophet.

crushed his body. The force was overwhelming. Unable to move and struggling to breathe, Muhammad felt certain he was about to die. Then he saw light like a dawning sun and heard a powerful voice: "Recite!"

Muhammad pleaded to know what to recite. The command sounded again, and the suffocating pressure increased. Suddenly, it stopped, and Muhammad heard these words: "Recite in the name of the Lord who created / Created humanity from a clot of blood."

More words followed in the form of poetry, so powerful that Muhammad felt the verses were being carved into his heart. When the words stopped, Muhammad fled from the cave and rushed to his wife Khadija, who wrapped him in a blanket. Muhammad trembled and wept. He finally told his wife about the encounter. "I think I have gone mad," he said.

Muhammad was inconsolable. Worried over her husband's distress, Khadija sought advice about the incident from a cousin. Khadija's cousin was Christian, and she recognized that Muhammad's experience was similar to those depicted in the Bible. She believed Muhammad had been given a message from Allah, or God—the creator of the world. "[Muhammad] is a prophet of this people," she told Khadija.

The year was about 610, and a major world religion—Islam—was about to be revealed. In the following months and years, Muhammad would continue to receive and recite

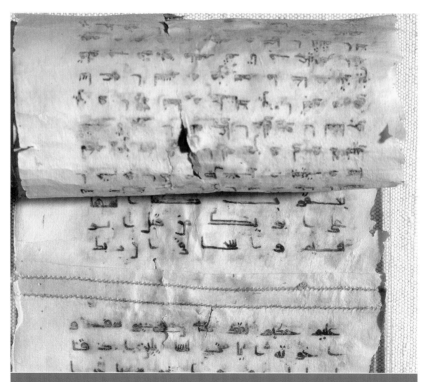

Followers of Islam later preserved Muhammad's recitations in writing. This scroll, made in Africa in the 800s, records Muhammad's message in Arabic.

the words of God. He would preach a new message to the Arabs—one that remade the way individuals related to each other and to God.

Muhammad attracted converts among the Arabs and established the first Islamic community. This community survived repeated efforts to destroy it. By the time of Muhammad's death in 632, the Islamic religion had spread across the Arabian Peninsula.

Under Muhammad's successors, Islam rolled out of the Middle East in a series of conquests. Arab Islamic armies conquered major empires. They unseated elites who had ruled for centuries. The changes brought by Islam were so sudden, extraordinary, and long-lasting that they still astonish. The borders and cultures established in this period of conquest still endure, more than thirteen hundred years later.

This book recounts the first hundred years of Islam. It is a story marked by passion, faith, bloodshed, ingenuity, and enlightenment. It is also a story about the origins of a civilization—one of the most dynamic and successful in history.

THE ORPHAN

According to tradition, Muhammad's birth coincided with a miracle. In A.D. 570, the Christian king of Yemen, a region on the southwestern tip of the Arabian Peninsula, plotted to attack Mecca and destroy its sacred shrine. The shrine, called the Kaaba, was the spiritual center of Arabia. There, people worshipped more than three hundred different gods. The king of Yemen wished to replace the Kaaba with a Christian church.

To give his army an advantage, the king imported a herd of elephants from Africa. These elephants terrified the Meccan defenders, who fled and left the way to the Kaaba open. Suddenly, an immense flock of birds carrying stones in their beaks appeared in the sky. Pelted by a shower of stones, the invaders were forced to retreat. Thus 570 became known as the Year of the Elephant. According to legend, it was also the year when an infant boy was born in the city and named Muhammad.

This Turkish painting from the late 1500s shows the king of Yemen's elephants surrounding the Kaaba.

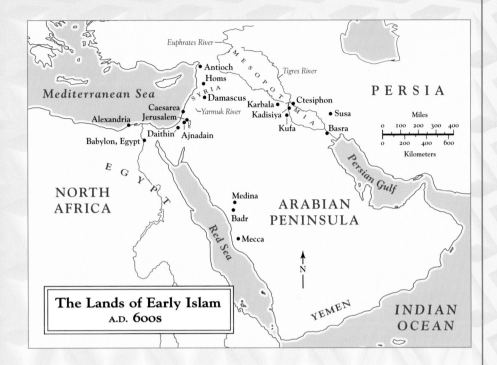

The Lands of Early Islam
A.D. 600s

Muhammad's early years were not easy. His father died before he was born. His mother died when he was six. The boy went to live with his grandfather, who died two years later. Having lost the three people closest to him before he was ten years old, Muhammad fell under the protection of his uncle Abu Talib.

Fortunately for Muhammad, Abu Talib was kind and generous. A trader, Abu Talib took the boy along with him on his trips north to Syria. In this era, traders traveled in groups called caravans. They used camels to carry trade goods. On trading journeys, the young Muhammad most likely saw the vast mixture of cultures and religions that made up Arabia and the surrounding lands of the Middle East.

THE ARABS

Muhammad's birth city, Mecca, is on the western edge of modern-day Saudi Arabia. That nation makes up most of the Arabian Peninsula, which sits at the heart of the Middle East. The region is mostly hot and dry. Much of the terrain is covered in sand or gravel. It is tough and unforgiving country.

WHEN WAS MUHAMMAD BORN?

No one knows Muhammad's exact birth date. The Arabs of Muhammad's time followed a lunar calendar, based on the movements of the moon. That calendar differs from the modern solar calendar, which is based on the movements of the sun. Because of this difference, scholars cannot date Muhammad's birth precisely. Some scholars speculate that early Islamic historians chose the year 570 for Muhammad's birth because it coincided with the miracle of the Year of the Elephant. (The exact date of the Year of the Elephant is also disputed.) In any case, Muhammad himself probably never knew the year of his birth, since birth dates were not important in early Arab culture. Most modern scholars agree that Muhammad was born sometime in the latter half of the sixth century.

In the A.D. 600s, the people of Arabia were mostly Arabs, an ethnic group bound together by a common culture and the Arabic language. Some Arabs lived in cities, such as Mecca. They made their living as traders and craftspeople. Other Arabs lived in small farming settlements clustered around oases—life-giving pools and wells of water. They used the water to irrigate their crops of dates and wheat.

Still other Arabs were nomads, people who move from place to place. The Arab nomads, called Bedouins, traveled to find plants and water for their animals. Some Bedouins raised sheep and goats, while others raised camels.

Camels are hardy creatures that can survive for two weeks without water. They can eat prickly bushes that grow in the dry desert soil. Traveling with camels, the Bedouins were able to penetrate deep into the Arabian deserts. A fourth-century Roman historian, Ammianus Marcellinus, described the Bedouin nomads this way: "No man ever grasps a plough handle nor cultivates a tree. They rove continually over wide and extensive tracts without a home, without fixed abodes or laws. They wander so widely that a woman marries in one place, gives birth in another, and rears her children far away."

The Bedouins were fierce warriors. Warfare, skirmishes, and raids were a part of their everyday lives. Bedouin men taught boys how to ride horses, aim a bow and arrow, and thrust with a sword. In the desert, all men had to know how to be soldiers.

As nomads, the Bedouins knew the Arabian interior intimately—its lonely paths and tiny, rare springs that bubbled beneath the sand. This knowledge offered them an enormous advantage against rivals and enemies. After a raid, the Bedouins could elude pursuers by disappearing into the desert. Only the foolish would follow them.

While the Bedouins left no paintings, sculpture, or buildings, they did produce a large body of art that was easily transportable—oral, or spoken, poetry. The Bedouins cherished great stories told well—stories of courage, love, and honor. In their desert camps, they gathered in the flickering light of campfires to listen to poets, who told of magnificent deeds in verse. In this passage, a poet describes a dawn raid:

We came upon them at dawn with our tall steeds, lean and sinewy and spears whose steel was as burning flame

And swords that reap the necks, keen and sharp of edge, kept carefully in the sheaths until the time of need

We came upon their host in the morning, and they were like a flock of sheep on whom falls the ravening wolf

We fell on them with white steel ground to keenness: we cut them to pieces until they were destroyed;

And we carried off their women on the saddles behind us, with their cheeks bleeding, torn by their nails in anguish.

MECCA—TRADING CENTER AND HOLY CITY

The Arabs were a crucial link in a vast trading network that knit together the large civilizations to the east and west. Arabia was in the center of this network. The peninsula's southern coast is on the Indian Ocean. On the northern side, roads led to the eastern Mediterranean Sea. Caravans loaded with incense from Africa; silk from China; and pepper, cloves, and other spices from India all traveled through Arabia.

The city of Mecca dominated the western area of the Arabian Peninsula. It served as a resting spot for caravans traveling north or south. It was close to the Red Sea and also near an oasis. Hills protected the city from pirate attacks from the sea, while the oasis provided water for travelers and their animals.

There was an even more important reason for visitors to stop in Mecca. The city was the site of the Kaaba shrine. The Kaaba is a cubelike structure made of low brick walls and a covering of cloth on top. Stories say that the Kaaba originally held a fragment of black meteorite that the Arabs considered holy. Eventually, it housed idols—images or small statues—representing 360 Arab gods. One of these gods was Allah. He oversaw the Kaaba and guaranteed peace to all visiting peoples.

The Kaaba became the holiest site in the Arab world. Every year, Arab pilgrims journeyed to Mecca for religious festivals. As part of the rituals, pilgrims circled the Kaaba several times on foot and touched sacred stones on the structure.

One tribe, or large group of families, ruled Mecca. This tribe, the Quraysh, benefited enormously from the Kaaba and from Mecca's location. The Kaaba gave the Quraysh prestige

The Kaaba sits at the center of Mecca in this painting of the city from the 800s. The city grew up around the walls and towers that surround the shrine.

in the Arab world. They made money from the pilgrims who visited the shrine during a three-month period every year. Mecca was also a center of trade. The Quraysh grew rich from trading festivals held during the same three-month period.

MUHAMMAD IN MECCA

In the 600s, Mecca and other Arabian cities had no police departments or town government as we know them in modern times. Rather, powerful tribes such as the Quraysh ruled the city. Clans, or extended families, protected their own. If someone insulted or injured one family member, the entire group took offense. After an insult, a family could be fanatical in its pursuit of revenge.

Certain people in Arab society, such as slaves, orphans, and the very poor, had no powerful family members to protect them. These people had little power or influence. Muhammad, an orphan, was fortunate that he had a caring uncle. He also benefited because he was a member of the powerful Quraysh tribe. Even so, Muhammad grew up knowing what it was like to be an outsider in Mecca.

Under his uncle's direction, Muhammad became a skillful trader. He developed a reputation for being both tough and principled. His skills attracted the attention of a rich widow named Khadija. She entrusted him to lead a caravan and to trade goods for her. When Muhammad returned to Mecca with a rich profit, she rewarded him with an offer of marriage. He accepted.

By the time Muhammad was middle-aged, he had become a successful, wealthy, and established merchant. Through his marriage to Khadija, he had children and a sizable fortune. In Mecca, he was respected for both his negotiating skills and his character.

Something was wrong, however. Muhammad was troubled. It is impossible to know Muhammad's exact thoughts at that time. He may have grown restless with the direction of his life, or perhaps he was disgusted with the excesses of Meccan society and culture. The rich and powerful ruled Mecca with little concern for the less fortunate—those without the protection of a tribe or clan.

THE QURAN

The Quran is the Islamic holy book. It consists of Allah's messages to Muhammad. The name *Quran* means "recitation" in Arabic. Originally, the Quran was not written down. Instead, a group called the Qurra—or Quran readers—memorized Muhammad's verses as he spoke them. Members of the Qurra traveled about the Islamic empire, reciting the verses and teaching them to others.

It may have distressed him that Arabs waged blood feuds over matters of insult and injury. For whatever reason, Muhammad sought solace in the cave on Mount Hira. There, he received a message from Allah.

And then there was silence. As if to test Muhammad's resolve, Allah did not speak to him for a long period after the first thunderous encounter. Muhammad doubted his sanity. Finally, the messages came again, reassuring him that he was not mad.

Over the next few years, Muhammad received poetic verses from Allah. The words came to him through the angel Gabriel. Many of these messages were joyful celebrations of the world and people. Others, however, called Meccans to do more for the poor, the weak, and the powerless. Taken together, the verses taught individuals how to relate to both God and other people. A new religion was coming to light through Muhammad.

At first, Muhammad revealed Allah's teachings only to his closest confidants and family members. His wife Khadija was his first convert. A thirteen-year-old cousin,

Ali, converted soon afterward. Abu Bakr, a friend and wealthy merchant, heard Muhammad and promptly gave away his fortune to the poor. Soon, Muhammad had thirty or forty followers.

Outside this group, however, Muhammad did not gain acceptance. He did not preach openly, so many people in Mecca didn't even know about his message. Other Meccans simply ignored him.

The Arab religious system was polytheist, meaning that most Arabs accepted the existence of many gods and goddesses. After three years, however, Muhammad began to threaten this system. He received new verses from Allah that carried a new tone. These messages said that Allah was the only god and that Muhammad was his messenger. Allah ordered Muhammad not to remain silent any longer. He told Muhammad to bring his message to the people.

MESSENGER OF GOD

At that time, Arabs mostly interacted with their gods by performing rituals. They asked the gods for protection or to grant their wishes. In return for favors, they offered specially prepared food and prayers to the gods. In these rituals, there was little sense of morality. That is, Arabs didn't ask: Is this act right or wrong? More likely, they asked whether it was permitted. For example, killing a person was perfectly acceptable in certain circumstances—for instance, to avenge an insult. But was killing another person itself wrong? None of the early Arab gods and goddesses demanded that people consider this question.

But Muhammad's teachings were very different. He preached that a person's life and actions had meaning. Muhammad spoke of a Last Day—a moment when everyone would be held accountable for their time on Earth. Nothing—not money, not power, not prestige—could protect someone from God's judgment.

"Who amasses wealth, hoarding it to himself / Does he really think his wealth will make him immortal?" asked Allah through Muhammad. Rather, acts of generosity—"To free a slave / To feed the destitute on a day of hunger / A kinsman orphan / Or a stranger out of luck in need"—would be remembered. Muhammad said that all people had an obligation to live moral lives and to care about everyone in the community—not just members of their own family or tribe.

Muhammad was uncompromising about the idea that Allah was the only god. He said that to communicate with Allah, one only had to recite and believe the verses that Allah had revealed through Muhammad. If this were true, then the Kaaba, crowded with the idols of many gods, was useless. If Muhammad was right, why would anyone make a pilgrimage to Mecca? For the Quraysh, this question struck at the source of their importance, power, and wealth.

Soon Meccans were heaping scorn, mistrust, and abuse on Muhammad. Some suspected that he was part of a plot from some other city or empire to seize control of Mecca's trading routes. Others said that Muhammad was a fortune teller, possessed by jinn, or spirits.

Despite the hostility, Muhammad continued to speak out. He urged his listeners to join him in his quest to serve the one true God. Although some Meccans ignored or criticized him, others listened. Muhammad's words were compelling to many, and so was Muhammad himself. He was firm and sincere when he preached, but he was also reasonable, generous, and kind. He did not rant like a fanatic. He earned respect and affection from important people in Meccan society—traders, warriors, and tribal leaders. Muhammad was comfortable in private conversations and in front of a large crowd. Through his charisma, he bound his followers to him personally as well as to his message.

BACKLASH

By 613 the Quraysh had begun to grow concerned. Muhammad wasn't an angry, isolated individual who could be easily dismissed. He was a successful and well-known businessman. He was also a member of the Quraysh tribe, which made his criticism more potent because it came from within Meccan society.

As Muhammad attracted more and more followers, Quraysh leaders grew more anxious and aggravated. The pilgrimage season was approaching. Muhammad planned to speak at the Kaaba to the thousands of pilgrims who would visit. How would it sound when Muhammad declared that the idols in the Kaaba were simply lifeless dolls and objects?

Quraysh leaders approached Muhammad's uncle, Abu Talib. They asked him to withdraw his protection from his nephew. This meant that if they attacked Muhammad, Talib would not seek revenge. Talib refused their request. Thwarted, the Quraysh then attempted to publicly discredit Muhammad. They described him as a sorcerer who used cunning words to break apart families and weaken the structure of society. They posted people on the roads into Mecca to warn approaching pilgrims about Muhammad.

The warnings had the opposite effect. Many pilgrims were intrigued by the controversy surrounding Muhammad. When Muhammad spoke at the Kaaba, he had a large audience—some of whom simply wanted to learn what all the fuss was about. When the pilgrims left Mecca and returned home, they carried Muhammad's message with them. Through discussions and arguments, the message started to spread throughout the Arabian Peninsula.

Then Muhammad was struck by personal tragedy. Within a short time, Abu Talib and Khadija both died. Khadija's death was a particularly devastating loss. She had been Muhammad's closest companion, a comfort and support to him during the moments when he had questioned himself and his sanity. Abu Talib had given Muhammad protection in Quraysh society. With his death, that protection was gone.

Members of the Quraysh quickly took advantage of the situation. They openly harassed and insulted Muhammad in the street. Once they even pelted him with stones. Threatened with physical harm, Muhammad could no longer remain in Mecca.

Muhammad looked outside the city for a place where he and his followers could practice their faith openly and in peace. But when Muhammad asked other tribes and towns if he could settle among them, they answered no. They did not want to anger the powerful Quraysh tribe. Finally, an invitation came from Yathrib, a collection of settlements around an oasis 250 miles (402 kilometers) north of Mecca.

MUHAMMAD AND HISTORY

We know very little about the historical Muhammad. Writers did not create any books or manuscripts about Muhammad during his lifetime. After his death, however, thousands of stories about him circulated among the Arabs. These stories are called traditions, or *hadith* in Arabic.

Some of the original traditions were not based on fact. People sometimes made them up to support a particular argument or perspective. (One man confessed to inventing four thousand traditions. He was executed for this crime.)

To separate the true hadith from the false, scholars in the centuries after Muhammad's death painstakingly traced the origin of each story. The true hadith became a key source of Islamic law. These stories reveal Muhammad's views on a number of issues. Scholars who can't resolve a problem using the Islamic holy book, the Quran, consult the hadith.

THE EXODUS

To avoid arousing suspicion, Muhammad's companions left Mecca in small groups over several days. This strategy worked. The Quraysh weren't even aware of the migration until only Muhammad, his cousin Ali, and his friend Abu Bakr were left in the city.

Believing that Muhammad would attempt to raise an army and return to attack Mecca, the leading families of the city sent a group of men armed with swords to slay Muhammad in his bed. Muhammad learned of the plot ahead of time and slipped out of the city with Abu Bakr. Ali remained behind as part of a ruse. He posed as Muhammad asleep. The assassins wasted several hours before they realized the trick. They did not harm Ali.

The Quraysh offered an enormous reward for Muhammad's capture. Dozens of Bedouin tribesmen looked for him in the surrounding desert. According to legend, Muhammad and Abu Bakr spent a night in a cave. There,

Abu Bakr (lower right, in white hat) *hides in a cave with* Muhammad (not shown) *as soldiers search outside. The painting comes from a Turkish book made around 1650.*

Allah had a spider spin webs across the entrance and a dove build a nest. When Muhammad's pursuers saw the web and the nest, they assumed that no one had entered the cave recently. They moved on.

Muhammad arrived safely in Yathrib, where a community of about sixty followers welcomed him joyfully. He entered the city on a camel, exhausted from his journey. Some residents took hold of the camel's reins and began to pull it to their house, promising Muhammad protection and food. But Muhammad ordered them to drop the reins. He did not want to show any group in Yathrib particular favor.

The camel walked unguided into an abandoned burial ground. There, it stopped and kneeled to allow Muhammad to dismount. On that site, Muhammad ordered that his followers build a mosque, or Islamic house of worship. Made out of mud bricks, it was the first mosque ever built.

Yathrib was later renamed Medinet al-Nabi, or the City of the Prophet. It is known in modern times by its shortened name—Medina. Muhammad's journey to Medina is called the Hegira. Islamic scholars later designated the year of this journey, 622, as the first year of the Islamic calendar.

CHAPTER TWO
MEDINA: CITY OF THE PROPHET

When the help of God arrived

And the opening

And you saw people joining the religion of God

In waves

Recite the praise of your lord.

—*Quran 110:1*

Medina became the place where Muhammad and his fewer than one hundred followers could at last freely practice their new religion. No longer did they have to pray or meet in secret or endure the harassment of their enemies in the streets of Mecca. In Medina the full extent of Muhammad's teachings began to emerge. His religion was not just a code or series of rituals by which to live. It offered a new vision of life itself.

At the time, Arab society valued status and wealth. When their personal or family pride had been wounded, people were expected to seek revenge. Muhammad's religion upended this worldview. Muhammad preached that people should be merciful instead of vengeful. He preached that everyone—even the wealthy—should be humble rather than proud.

This map, created by an Arab geographer in Sicily around 1150, shows Mecca (bottom) and Medina (top) and the Red Sea. The map's orientation is different from modern-day maps, with north at the bottom instead of at the top.

Muhammad described the typical Arab attitude as *kufr*, which means "ingratitude" or "denial." He said that this attitude should be replaced by *islam*, or "submission" to God. Those who submitted to Allah and believed Muhammad to be his messenger became known as Muslims, "those who submit" to God.

Muhammad was concerned about both individuals and the larger community. After all, it was difficult for people to worship God properly if the community mocked their ideals and offered temptations to deviate from God's message. In Medina, Muhammad taught people how to worship together in the mosque. Muhammad also stressed the importance of following the laws of Islam in private life—for example, by praying alone several times a day.

MEDINA VERSES AND MECCA VERSES

The verses Muhammad received in Mecca, from 610 to 622, were universal in nature. They addressed the general state of people and their relationship to each other and to God. After Muhammad moved to Medina, the tone of the verses he received changed. In Medina, the verses addressed specific questions and problems that the first Islamic community encountered in their daily lives. Later, Islamic historians and scholars closely examined the Medina community to gain a better understanding of these verses.

ESTABLISHING POWER IN MEDINA

Before Muhammad arrived in Medina, its tribes had been locked in an ugly and bitter rivalry. Realizing that they could not find a solution among themselves, the Medina tribes had asked the outsider Muhammad to mediate their disputes. The fact that Muhammad came from the Quraysh tribe enhanced his prestige and gave him credibility.

It soon became clear, however, that Muhammad had no intention of simply ruling on tribal disputes. In 622 he and the Medina tribes agreed to the Oath of Aqaba. Not only did the oath recognize Muhammad's position as the ultimate judge in the community (a position called shaykh), it also acknowledged him as the Prophet of Allah.

This oratory, or prayer room, stands near Mecca. It marks the place where the Medina tribes agreed to Muhammad's leadership.

In addition, Muhammad began to insist that the tribes of Medina live according to Islamic moral laws. These are laws about right and wrong. Frequently, because food was scarce, families abandoned infants they couldn't care for—especially female infants, since males were more prized. Muhammad forbade this practice. He also declared that slaves should be treated humanely and that they be allowed to marry. (One of Muhammad's first converts was a slave, whom he promptly freed.) Not everyone was pleased by the new laws. One resident of Medina, Abu Afak, complained that "here is a rider come among them who has divided them, [saying] 'This is permitted; this is forbidden' to all kinds of things."

Muhammad emphasized the equality of all souls before God. According to Arab tradition at the time, when a person of lower status committed an insult or crime against a person of higher status, the punishment was more severe than if a person of higher status committed a crime against a person of lower status. Muhammad made the penalty equal, regardless of who had committed a crime against whom. Muhammad also insisted that each member of the Muslim community pay a tax—called a *zakat*—that was distributed to the poor.

WAR WITH MECCA

Secure in Medina, Muhammad turned his attention back to Mecca. He ordered attacks on caravans to threaten the livelihood of the Meccan traders. After several successful raids, the Quraysh sent an army to destroy Muhammad and his movement. Though heavily outnumbered, Muhammad and his tiny band routed this force at the Battle of Bedr. The victory enhanced Muhammad's power and prestige throughout the Arabian Peninsula.

To avenge their defeat, the Meccans sent another army to Medina the following year. In this battle, Muhammad and his forces fought on foot and out in the open. The Meccans overwhelmed them. In the course of battle, Muhammad was bloodied and wounded. One of his last surviving companions dragged Muhammad to the shelter of a gorge. News spread that Muhammad was dead. The fighting abruptly ceased, and the Quraysh army roared cheers of victory. Muhammad and his remaining men, defeated but still alive, managed to retreat to their settlement in Medina.

Muhammad's army clashes with the Meccan army in 625 at the Battle of Uhud, in which Muhammad was wounded. This painting comes from a Turkish book made around 1600.

Muhammad tended to his wounds and rebuilt his community. After two years, the Quraysh again tried to crush the Muslims. They raised their largest army yet and marched on Medina. This time, Muhammad remained in a fortified area within the city. He was not going to risk another defeat by fighting the Quraysh army in the open. His soldiers dug a massive trench that separated the two armies. During the following Battle of the Trench, neither force could gain an advantage. After a month of inconclusive skirmishing, the Quraysh army exhausted its supplies and withdrew.

NETWORKING

After the battle, Muhammad continued his efforts to knit the Arab tribes together under Islam. He converted some tribes and made alliances with others, especially Christian tribes. Those who completely refused to cooperate were dealt with through force. This treatment was rare, however, as Muhammad preferred to reason and explain his message rather than fight. "Deal gently and not harshly," he told one of his messengers. "Announce good news and do not repel people."

Muhammad's efforts resulted in a political network across Arabia that rivaled the system of the Quraysh. Muhammad's system offered the benefits of peace and unity. No tribe that was allied with Muhammad could attack another allied tribe. In addition, Muhammad acted as a judge to settle intertribal disputes.

Muhammad wished to extend his system north into Syria, a rich and fertile land inhabited by many Arabs. Most were Christians who had sworn allegiance to the vast Byzantine

Empire (based in modern-day Turkey). If Muhammad could gain their support, he could cut Mecca off from north-south trading routes—threatening the Quraysh financially.

As Muhammad grew stronger, the Quraysh weakened. One year after the Battle of the Trench, Muhammad and one thousand of his followers marched unarmed and peacefully to Mecca to take part in the annual pilgrimage at the Kaaba. Muhammad meant to demonstrate the size of his community and at the same time show that they could be peaceful and civilized.

The Quraysh were desperate to prevent Muhammad from entering Mecca. After several meetings outside the city, Muhammad and the Quraysh agreed to a truce. The agreement ended hostilities between the two groups and also delayed Muhammad's pilgrimage for a year. Dealing from a position of strength, Muhammad did not have to agree to the treaty. Nonetheless, he thought it was a prudent political move. Muhammad and his pilgrims went back to Medina.

They returned the following year and this time entered Mecca. The Quraysh had portrayed Muhammad as a villain and sorcerer. But this description contrasted directly with the image of Muhammad and fellow Muslims walking peacefully through the city's streets to the Kaaba. The peaceful display impressed many Meccans and won Muhammad more converts.

COERCION AND CONVERSION

In 630 Muhammad accused the Quraysh of breaking their peace treaty. This time, he returned to Mecca with a giant army. The city could do nothing but surrender. Muhammad, who had fled Mecca eight years before as the leader of a tiny band, had returned as its conqueror. He entered the Kaaba with Ali and took out the idols one by one. In full sight of the city, he smashed them to the ground. The Kaaba was then dedicated to Allah alone—the one God.

Some of the Meccans and Muhammad's followers may have been astonished that Muhammad's only acts of destruction were to the idols in the Kaaba. At that time, tribes that lost wars usually suffered terribly. Conquering soldiers often executed the men, looted homes, and sold the women and children into slavery. Muhammad had endured bitter persecution from many Meccans. According to pre-Islamic Arab culture, it was natural that he would seek revenge. Muhammad, however, treated the people with forgiveness.

With his victory in Mecca, Muhammad had become a dominant figure on the Arabian Peninsula. Delegation after delegation of Arab tribes came to Medina to negotiate peace with him. On one occasion, a group of delegates dressed in silk robes and glistening with gold jewelry arrived in Muhammad's tent. Muhammad ignored them. Ali explained that Muhammad disdained clothing and jewelry that showed off wealth. When the delegates appeared the next day in simple white robes, Muhammad invited them to sit with him.

If tribal leaders agreed to convert to Islam, Muhammad treated them generously. If they insisted on the worship of idols, however, Muhammad ordered his generals to speak to them about Islam for three days. The offer went something like this:

If you refuse [to convert to Islam], you must pay the tribute [tax]. This is a bad thing but not as bad as the alternative; if you refuse to pay, it will be war. If you respond positively and embrace our religion, we shall leave you with the book of God and teach you its contents. Provided that you govern according [to] the rules included in it, we shall leave your country and let you deal with its affairs as you please. If you protect yourself against us by paying the tribute, we will accept it from you and guarantee your safety. Otherwise we shall fight you.

Given these choices—conversion, taxes, or war—many tribal leaders converted.

JEWS AND CHRISTIANS

Muhammad was not the first to introduce monotheism—or worshipping only one god—to the Middle East. Judaism and Christianity are also monotheistic religions. By the 600s, these religions were long established in the Middle East as well as in Europe.

In many ways, Muhammad saw Islam not as a new religion but rather a continuation of Judaism and Christianity. Muhammad saw himself as the final prophet in a long line of prophets described in Jewish and Christian scriptures.

In this spirit, Muhammad preached that Muslims should be tolerant of Judaism and Christianity. Jews and Christians, he said, were "people of the book" (the Jewish Torah and the Christian Bible). All stood before the same one God. Allah had previously sent prophets to Jews and Christians, and at last also to the Arabs. Muhammad stated repeatedly that no Jew or Christian should be forced to convert to Islam.

It is important to note, however, that Islam did not mesh seamlessly with Judaism and Christianity. While Muhammad openly respected these religions, he also saw their followers as people who in some ways had lost the true path to God. For example, Muhammad said that the Christian belief that

This 1850 painting from India shows Christians approaching a flame, which symbolizes Muhammad, for advice. Islamic tradition discourages realistic portraits of prophets, especially Muhammad. Religious artists often show him as a veiled figure or a flame.

God, Jesus, and the Holy Spirit were all one was a dangerous falsehood. Muhammad preached that God had sent him to correct the older monotheisms that had been corrupted over time. Islam, in this view, was the final and most advanced form of monotheism.

THE SCANDAL OF THE NECKLACE

Not everything went smoothly for Muhammad during this period, especially in his private life. Muhammad had had a long marriage with Khadija. The couple had six children, four of whom survived to adulthood. It was common for Arab men to have more than one wife, but Muhammad took no other woman to be his wife while Khadija was alive.

After Khadija's death, Muhammad married several women. These marriages, for the most part, were not based on love. Instead, Muhammad married for political and other reasons. For instance, he married the daughters of powerful men to establish and protect alliances. He married an elderly widow to set the example that those who were well off should provide for the poor.

One of Muhammad's wives was Aisha, his friend Abu Bakr's daughter. Aisha always accompanied Muhammad on his trips. One day after a raid, Aisha left the campsite and lost a necklace that Muhammad had given her. While she searched for it, the caravan moved on, not realizing that Aisha had been left behind.

Aisha was suddenly alone in the desert. A young Arab man—a childhood friend—accidentally discovered her. They both realized their dilemma. The man could not leave

Aisha in the desert, where she might die. On the other hand, if he spent time with her alone, it might ignite rumors of infidelity.

The man made his choice. He pulled her up onto his camel behind him and rode off in search of the caravan. He caught up to it the next morning. By then, Aisha's absence had been discovered. Muhammad was frantic with worry. Aisha's arrival, however, brought new problems. The

MOTHERS AND DAUGHTERS

The women in Muhammad's life played an important role in Islam. Muhammad's wives are collectively called the Mothers of the Believers. In modern times, they are considered role models for Muslim women. Muhammad had four daughters from his marriage to Khadija. One of them, Fatima *(right, veiled)*, married Muhammad's cousin Ali *(right)*. She gave birth to two sons, Hasan and Husayn *(right front)*, who would become the central figures of the Shiite branch of Islam. In the modern Muslim world, Fatima is among the most popular names for females.

whole camp gossiped about Aisha riding on a camel with a handsome young man after a night alone.

Muhammad's opponents were soon spreading racy verses about the incident. Muhammad himself believed that Aisha had been faithful, but the scandal was fracturing the community. Some thought Muhammad should divorce Aisha. When he asked Aisha to repent for her sins, Aisha replied that there was nothing to be forgiven. Infuriated, she moved out of Muhammad's lodgings and returned to her mother.

Most of Muhammad's closest friends thought she had been unfaithful, but only Ali stated publicly that Muhammad should divorce her. This advice earned Ali the enmity of Aisha's father, Abu Bakr.

In the end, Muhammad did not divorce Aisha. While meditating on the affair, he received a verse from God that proclaimed Aisha's innocence. Overjoyed, he told the news to Aisha. "To God's praise and your blame!" she shot back, angered that he hadn't believed her in the first place. Aisha and Muhammad were reconciled, but the split between Aisha and Ali would never be.

CHAPTER THREE
THE FIRST CALIPH

I have been given authority over you, although I am not the best of you. If I do well, help me; and if I do wrong, set me right. . . . Obey me for so long as I obey God and His Messenger. But if I disobey God and His Messenger, you owe me no obedience.

—Abu Bakr, 632, addressing his congregation after Muhammad's death

In 632 Muhammad was struck with a fever that left him too weak to leave his house for several days. He rested in Aisha's room. On the tenth day, he struggled out of bed when he heard the call to morning prayers. When prayers were over, he returned to his house. Finally, he murmured, "Lord, grant me pardon." Then he died.

News of Muhammad's death spread among the Muslim community, evoking shock and pain. One follower, Umar, refused to believe the news. He shouted that Muhammad had gone alive to heaven like other prophets and would soon return. He threatened to beat anyone who spoke of Muhammad being dead, adding that he would cut off their hands and feet as punishment when Muhammad returned. Abu Bakr, who had seen the body, urged Umar to be quiet. Confronted with the reality that Muhammad was gone, Umar collapsed and wept.

No one at first knew what to do. Muhammad had not openly proclaimed a successor. Muhammad's closest supporters—called the companions—were fearful and divided. Who would lead the Muslim community now that the Prophet was gone?

ALI VERSUS ABU BAKR

Many believed the new leader should be Ali. Ali was one of Muhammad's closest friends, his cousin, the husband of his daughter Fatima, and possibly his first male believer. Ali's sons were the only male descendants of the Prophet. When Muhammad had emptied the idols from the Kaaba, only Ali had helped him. Ali was also one of Islam's great warriors. After one battle, Muhammad called him "the lion that returns again and again to the fight." When Muhammad died, Ali expressed his grief in poetry, saying "the entire world is now dark without you." Ali's supporters claimed that Muhammad had designated Ali to be the next leader of the Muslim community.

Others, however, supported Abu Bakr. Three years younger than Muhammad, Abu Bakr had been the first male

This portrait of Abu Bakr appears in a Persian history of the world from around 1310.

adult convert to Islam. In accordance with Islamic beliefs, he had given much of his fortune to the poor. When Muhammad had fled Mecca to escape assassination, Abu Bakr had been the one companion who accompanied him. In Medina, Abu Bakr gave the remaining portion of his wealth to purchase land for the first mosque. Called "the truthful" or "the sincere," Abu Bakr was widely respected within the Muslim community. Shortly before his death, Muhammad had designated Abu Bakr to lead the community in prayer. Abu Bakr's supporters stated that with this act, Muhammad had publicly passed on his leadership to Abu Bakr.

Abu Bakr was completely loyal to Muhammad and Islam. One story describes a conversation between Abu Bakr and his eldest son. The son had fought for the Meccans in some of the first battles against the Muslims. After the son later converted to Islam, he told his father: "I found you twice under my sword at [the Battle of] Bedr, but I could not raise my hand [to kill you] because of my love for you." Abu Bakr replied: "If I had had the chance I would have killed you."

The dispute over Ali and Abu Bakr was more than just a debate about the personal qualities of the two men. Ali was a member of the Prophet's clan. If he became the new leader, power might pass to another relative after his death. Abu Bakr's supporters saw this as a dangerous precedent— with only descendants of Muhammad's clan being eligible to lead the Muslim community. Abu Bakr's supporters also worried that Muhammad's descendants might try to rule on religious as well as secular (nonreligious) issues. Thus, too much power would end up in the hands of just one clan. Abu Bakr and his followers were determined to prevent this situation.

ABU BAKR SEIZES POWER

The period immediately after Muhammad's death was marked by confusion. According to historical accounts, Ali washed Muhammad's body for burial. After three days, Ali supposedly buried the body beneath Muhammad's tent. Many historians are surprised by this act, since the early Arabs rarely, if ever, buried bodies among the living. Some believe that Ali buried the body to prevent his rivals from leading a funeral procession and in that way claiming authority over the Muslim community.

After Muhammad's burial, Abu Bakr and a group of men from Mecca came to Medina. They arrived just as local leaders began debating who should be Muhammad's successor. The Medina men were determined to pick a leader from among themselves. Abu Bakr chose this moment to speak. While Abu Bakr praised the men from Medina, he also reminded them that Islam had by then spread throughout the peninsula and that only a man from Mecca could retain the loyalty of the newly converted Arab tribes.

When a Medina man suggested that each group select its own leader, Umar roared, "Who will willingly take precedence [first place] over the man that the Prophet ordered to lead the prayer?" In the silence that followed, Umar raised Abu Bakr's hand and pledged allegiance to him. The others soon followed. The Muslim community had a new leader. Abu Bakr was called *caliph,* or "successor" to Muhammad.

The next morning, Islam's first caliph, Abu Bakr, addressed the congregation at the mosque:

> I have been given authority over you, although I am not the best of you. If I do well, help me; and if I do wrong, set me right. Truth consists in loyalty and disregard of truth is treachery. The weak among you shall be strong in my eyes until I have secured his rights, if God wills it. And the strong among you shall be weak with me until I have wrested from him the rights of others, if God wills it. Obey me for so long as I obey God and His Messenger. But if I disobey God and His Messenger, you owe me no obedience.

Abu Bakr's move was very daring. He had acted quickly and without securing the support of other prominent

Muslims. The Muslim community learned that it had a new leader only after the fact was already accomplished.

Ali remained in his tent over the next few months, refusing to acknowledge Abu Bakr's new authority. When he did speak to Abu Bakr, he complained, "You did confront us with a thing accomplished, leaving us no say in the matter." Furthermore, Ali said that he and other relatives of Muhammad should be the ones to lead Islam. "We felt that we had some claim as the nearest in kinship to the Messenger of God," he argued.

Ali eventually acknowledged Abu Bakr as the caliph. The two men came to an agreement, which they demonstrated by worshipping together publicly at the mosque. The split between the two men, however, would never truly heal. It would widen over the history of Islam, becoming the basis for the modern Sunni–Shiite divide. In modern times, Islam is split into two main branches: Sunni and Shiite. The Shiites (the smaller group) believe that a duplicitous agreement denied Ali his rightful place at the head of the Muslim community.

WHO WAS WITH MUHAMMAD?

The Shiites and Sunnis remember Muhammad's death differently. The Shiites believe that Muhammad was leaning against Ali's shoulder when he died. The Sunnis believe that he died with his head cradled in his wife Aisha's lap.

This story involves more than just a struggle for political power, however. Abu Bakr and Ali had possibly hated each other since the scandal over Aisha's necklace. After Abu Bakr became caliph, he stripped Ali and his family of their inheritance from Muhammad. Abu Bakr claimed that Muhammad wanted to leave no property to his descendants, just handouts of food and clothing from the Muslim community. While Ali accepted the decision, his wife Fatima was distressed at losing both her father and her inheritance. She died a short time later.

SUBMISSION, EXILE, OR THE SWORD

As the new caliph, Abu Bakr faced pressing problems. Some non-Muslim Arab tribes, learning of Muhammad's death, moved quickly to assert their independence. With Muhammad dead, they no longer believed they should have to pay a special tax to the Muslims. Other tribes were willing to keep paying the tax, but only if they could be independent of Medina's control.

In addition to these challenges, a number of prophet figures appeared in Arabia. These individuals copied Muhammad, setting up communities of believers and claiming they spoke directly with God. In eastern Arabia, a tribe following a prophet named Maslama suggested that Arabia be divided into two, one for the Muslims and one for the followers of Maslama.

Abu Bakr knew this political threat had to be answered with a combination of force and diplomacy. He moved quickly. He crushed a small tribal insurrection and then returned to

THE ULEMA

As caliph, Abu Bakr avoided ruling on religious questions. He let religious scholars called *ulemas* ("those with knowledge") rule on such debates. In modern times, ulemas still carry out this role. The ulemas have no official leader. They debate questions concerning Islamic law and Muslim society among themselves. At times, the ulemas have clashed with Muslim political rulers over matters of power and Islamic law. For the most part, however, the two groups have kept their roles separate.

Medina. He sent riders throughout the peninsula on a special mission. Their message was forgiving but firm. Any tribe who repented and swore allegiance to Abu Bakr and the Muslim state would be pardoned. Anyone who didn't would be dealt with severely. According to Islamic history, Abu Bakr gave the tribes three options: "submission, exile, or the sword."

As the messengers entered each village and delivered Abu Bakr's ultimatum, Muslim cavalry waited nearby. If the cavalrymen didn't hear the call to prayer the next morning—signaling submission to Islam—they attacked the village, killed the men, trampled the crops, and took the women and children captive.

Abu Bakr kept the core of his battle-hardened army to confront the Arab tribes who offered the most resistance. One by one, these tribes were defeated and absorbed in a series of sharp conflicts called the Ridda Wars. The word *ridda* means "rejection of Islam."

Following Muhammad's example, Abu Bakr urged his soldiers to follow specific rules when waging war: "Do not kill women or children, or an aged infirm person. Do not cut down fruit-bearing trees. Do not destroy an inhabited place. Do not slaughter sheep or camels except for food. Do not burn bees and do not scatter them." Within two years, Abu Bakr had not only reclaimed all the territory that had been Islamic at Muhammad's death, he had also doubled Islamic territory to include almost all of the Arabian Peninsula.

CALL TO ARMS

By then, almost all Arabia—even the Bedouins of the desert— had become Islamic. This stability, however, led to a problem. Muhammad had opposed the routine use of violence—raids, vendettas, and blood feuds—among Arab tribes. Muslims, said Muhammad, needed to respect other Muslims.

But in Bedouin culture, raiding and warfare were a part of everyday life. Abu Bakr knew it would be difficult to insist that the Bedouins suddenly give up fighting and settle into a peaceful existence. Rather than fight each other, however, Abu Bakr directed the tribes to look outward—to direct their fierce energy toward outside enemies.

Abu Bakr called on Muslim men throughout Arabia to join a campaign to spread Islam. Messengers on horses sped to the tribes, carrying the caliph's appeal on pieces of parchment marked with black writing. The letters were sealed with wax, impressed with the insignia of Muhammad's ring—one of the few artifacts Muhammad had left behind.

When a messenger arrived, the tribal leader gave him a bowl of fresh milk—a traditional gesture of welcome. The tribal leader then kissed the seal, broke it, and read the contents of the letter to the adult male members of the tribe.

Young Muslim men answered the call eagerly by gathering at Medina. Abu Bakr ordered them to march north. The army moved in three columns, while a fourth unit of soldiers, fresh from successful fighting near the Euphrates River, moved from the west to join them. These were tough soldiers who knew how to fight. One poet, a contemporary of Muhammad, sang:

Truly War knows that I am her child

And that I am the chief who wears her token in fight.

And that I dwell on a mountain top of glory in the highest honor

And that I render restive and distress

Mail-clad warriors in the black dust of battle.

And that I dash upon them when they flinch before me,

In an attack more fierce than the springing of a lion.

The Arab culture was united under Islam. Through Muhammad, Allah had promised that those who died fighting for Islam would be rewarded in heaven: "Let those

THE FIRST CALIPH

47

fight in the path of God who sell the life of this world for the other. Whoever fights in the path of God, whether he be killed or be victorious, on him shall We bestow a great reward." The Arab conquests had begun.

THE OPENING PHASE

The typical Arab Muslim army in the seventh century had about four thousand men. Most were simple foot soldiers. The army also had cavalry—soldiers who rode horses. Camels were used to carry supplies.

Both the Arab soldiers and their enemies had similar types of equipment. The weapon of choice was the sword, which had a straight double-edged blade about three feet long. The sword hung over a soldier's shoulder in a leather or wooden sheath. The sword was the pride of the Arab soldier. Some heroes even named their swords.

Many soldiers also carried spears, which varied in size. The longer ones had metal heads mounted on wooden poles and were designed to stab and slash. Other, shorter spears were designed to be thrown. In addition to spears and swords, many Arab soldiers carried small bows that could launch arrows hundreds of yards.

For protection, the typical Arab soldier carried a shield, probably a small circular disk made of wood and covered with leather. Metal armor and helmets (nicknamed eggs by the Arab soldiers) were much rarer, since metal was expensive. Metal armor was an especially sought-after prize of war.

Traditionally, each Arab army was led by a champion— its strongest warrior. Battles between two armies started with

Arab foot soldiers carry spears, swords, and round shields into battle against Greek opponents. This Sicilian illustration from a thirteenth-century copy of the Scylitzes Chronicle *shows an 870 battle.*

the champions challenging each other to individual combat. Finally, the two armies joined the contest. The battle descended into a chaotic swirl of individuals hacking and stabbing each other.

The Arab armies marching north, however, had evolved into a more organized force. The Arabs fought with cavalry at the front, followed by one or two lines of archers. After the archers came the infantry, divided into three groups—on the left, on the right, and in the center. The generals leading these armies came from either Mecca or Medina. Soldiers knew their generals by sight and could often spot them fighting on the battlefield.

In the early years, Muslim soldiers were not paid in cash. They divided up booty—armor, swords, jewels, gold, and slaves—captured from the people they conquered. They were required to send one-fifth of this loot to Mecca to be distributed to the Muslim community.

THE EASTERN ROMAN EMPIRE

Heading north, the Arabs confronted an empire with a history and religion that stretched back centuries. In A.D. 457, the Roman Empire had partially collapsed after attacks by tribes from northern and eastern Europe. The European, or western, portion of the Roman Empire fell into a period of decay. Historians later called this period of European history the Dark Ages.

The rich provinces of the eastern half of the Roman Empire, however, remained strong. Called the Byzantine Empire, this empire covered modern-day Turkey, Syria, Israel, Palestine, and Egypt. Its capital city was Constantinople (modern-day Istanbul, Turkey). The empire had a population between 17 and 27 million people. The ruling class spoke Greek.

By the 600s, several factors had left the Byzantine Empire vulnerable to foreign attack. First, Christianity was the dominant religion in the empire. But people in different parts of the empire had their own views about Christianity. For instance, they disagreed about the nature of Jesus, whose teachings form the basis for Christianity. Christian groups clashed with one another, and all efforts to compromise failed. Finally, the Byzantine government forced everyone to accept one type of Christianity. In some places, people bitterly resisted, causing their leaders to begin a harsh and bloody crackdown. The disagreements over religion tore at the empire's unity.

Further weakening the Byzantines, a deadly disease—plague—ravaged the empire in the last half of the sixth century. The plague reduced the empire's population by as much as one-third. But by far the greatest drain on the Byzantine Empire was a series of ruinous wars waged with the neighboring Persian Empire, centered in modern-day Iran.

A particularly bloody and destructive phase in the Byzantine–Persian rivalry began in the early 600s. At that time, the succession to the Byzantine throne was contested. A series of savage assassinations brought unrest and instability to the empire. The Persian emperor, hoping to take advantage of the chaos, invaded the Byzantine Empire from the east. Persian armies brought the war almost to the gates of Constantinople. They overwhelmed Syria and Palestine and entered Egypt.

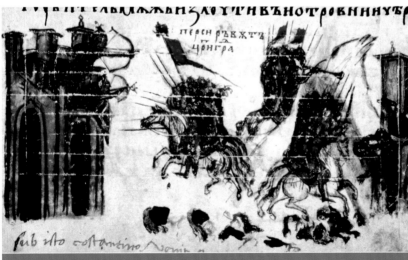

The Persian army attacks Byzantine forces outside Constantinople in 626. The image comes from a 1300s Slavonic copy of a Greek history from the late 1100s.

This patch shows Byzantine emperor Heraclius riding into battle with horse and spear. The embroidered image appeared on an Egyptian tunic from the late 700s.

Under Emperor Heraclius's direction, the Byzantine Empire counterattacked and invaded Persia. In 628 Heraclius at last ended the twenty-five-year war in triumph. "The haughty enemy of God [the Persian emperor] has fallen," he proclaimed. "He has fallen and tumbled into the depths, and his name has been obliterated from the earth. . . . His labor turned against him, and his wrongfulness came down on his head." Heraclius, by then age fifty-three, prepared to enjoy the fruits of peace.

WINNING THE WAR, LOSING THE PEACE

For many years, the Byzantine Empire had made payments to buy the loyalty of the Arab tribes on its southern border. These tribes—the Ghassani—had formed a buffer between the empire's frontier and the other tribes of the Arabian Peninsula. The allied Arab tribes protected a 100-mile-deep (161 km) frontier zone. In the case of invasion, they could repel an initial attack, alert the Byzantine army, and buy time for the larger Byzantine forces to prepare for battle.

During the sixth and early seventh centuries, this defensive policy had been effective. The Arabs knew the local area—the hidden trails and the main routes—as well as the people who lived there. After the war with Persia ended, however, the Byzantine Empire cut off payments to its Arab allies. Relations between the empire and the Ghassani were broken.

Worse for the Byzantines, the long wars with Persia had exhausted and weakened their empire. The loss of its Arab allies in the south left it exposed. What's more, without its Arab allies, the empire had almost no information about the dramatic change that had occurred in Arabia.

MARCHING TOWARD BYZANTIUM

In 634 an Arab Muslim army under the command of Amr ibn al-As entered southern Palestine. The local Byzantine commander, Sergios, soon learned of this invasion. He led three hundred soldiers to attack Amr's army. The Arab Muslims routed this force at Dathin. Sergios was killed.

The shock of the defeat spread through Palestine. Sergios

had been a high-ranking Byzantine official with access to the emperor himself. Although the battle was probably little more than a large skirmish, the death of Sergios was significant.

After Dathin, the Byzantines' southern border was left open to Muslim raiding parties. A larger Byzantine army rapidly rushed south and confronted the invaders. In the meantime, another Muslim army appeared. This one was led by Khalid ibn al-Walid, who had marched five hundred men through a barren desert in Mesopotamia (modern-day Iraq). This feat surprised the Byzantines, as the desert was considered virtually impregnable.

Khalid, who would become known as the Sword of God for his exploits on the battlefield, captured a Syrian city and then hurried south to join Amr. Amr and Khalid's united force defeated a large Byzantine army at Ajnadayn. This defeat left all of Palestine and southern Syria open to Muslim invasion. According to one chronicle, the Muslim

KHALID'S MARCH

Khalid's march through the desert has long passed into legend. One story says that Khalid and his men had to travel for six days through dry terrain. To enable his men to survive the journey, Khalid forced his camels to drink more water than normal. Then he muzzled their mouths closed. Each day on the march, his thirsty men slaughtered some of the camels and drank the water from their stomachs.

commanders offered Emperor Heraclius the chance to buy back the booty they had seized from his defeated forces. Heraclius refused.

The remaining Byzantine forces fled to the protection of walled towns. The Muslim Arab armies moved into the countryside around them, causing havoc to intercity trade and relations. On Christmas 634, Christian residents of Jerusalem were unable to visit nearby Bethlehem, the birthplace of Jesus, because the road had been blocked. "The army of the godless [Muslims] has captured the divine

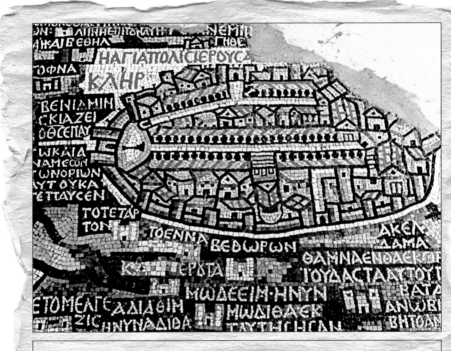

This mosaic from Madaba, Jordan, shows Jerusalem and the many small towns that the Muslim army would have occupied. Created around 550, the mosaic is the oldest surviving map of Christian holy places.

Bethlehem and bars our passage there, threatening slaughter and destruction if we leave this holy city and dare approach our beloved and sacred Bethlehem," wrote Sophronius, the powerful Christian patriarch (leader) of Jerusalem.

Sophronius was a man of deep education and experience. He had lived in various cities of the Byzantine Empire, in both the east and the west. However, he had little understanding of the Arab armies that had appeared out of nowhere to threaten Byzantine rule. To Sophronius, they were an agent of God's will, a punishment inflicted on Christians for being lax and immoral.

God's will or not, he prayed for their destruction. "If we repent for our sins," he wrote, "we will laugh at the demise of our enemies and in short time we will see their destruction and complete ruin. For their bloody swords will pierce their own hearts, their bows will be splintered, their arrows will be left sticking in them and they will open the way to Bethlehem for us."

It was a grim winter for the Byzantines. While few cities fell immediately to the Muslim armies, the Byzantine forces failed to make a coordinated defense or counterattack. Moreover, the cities were soon crowded with refugees from the countryside, who were panicked and needed food and shelter.

Muslim forces surrounded the major city of Damascus in Syria. After a time (probably several months, although historians aren't sure), the city surrendered in 635. Its mostly Christian Arab population may have felt more kinship with the Muslim Arab invaders than with the Byzantine authorities. In any case, it appears that the city

Abu Bakr (right) and his successor Umar meet in a garden in the afterlife. Created in India in 1686, this painting illustrates a poem about the Muslim caliphs.

surrendered peacefully. Muslim soldiers did not disturb the inhabitants.

As these victories were being reported, Abu Bakr was struck with fever. Realizing that the disease might kill him, he assembled the companions and bid them accept his nominee for succession—Umar. This move effectively prevented Ali and his supporters from making a bid for caliph. Ali, once again, had been left out.

CHAPTER FOUR
GREAT VICTORIES UNDER UMAR

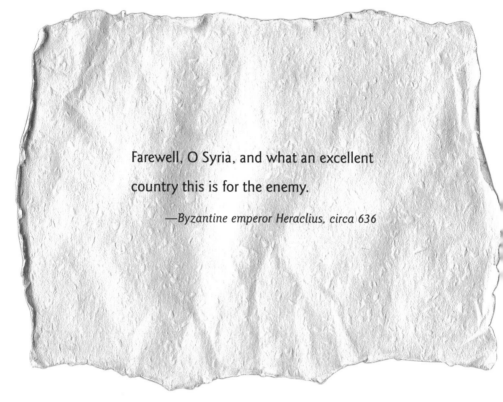

Farewell, O Syria, and what an excellent country this is for the enemy.

—*Byzantine emperor Heraclius, circa 636*

Umar, the new caliph, had first won fame as a wrestler. Tall and completely bald, in a crowd he "towered above the people as if he were on horseback." In Mecca he had first regarded the spread of Islam with disgust and had publicly announced that he would kill Muhammad. Someone suggested that if he was going to fight Islam, he should start in his own house. Umar rushed home, where he discovered his sister and brother-in-law reciting portions of the

Quran—Allah's messages to Muhammad. Enraged, he beat them. Finally, exhausted, he asked them about what they had been reciting. After hearing a verse, he was enticed and then converted.

The companions were at first unenthusiastic about Umar's leadership because he was known for being severe and harsh. But Abu Bakr argued that the responsibility of leadership would soften Umar's tough personality. Abu Bakr's logic persuaded the companions, who agreed to Umar as the next caliph. Abu Bakr died a few days later.

ONE OF GOD'S BATTLES

As the Muslims pledged their allegiance to Umar, Heraclius, emperor of the Byzantines, was preparing to confront the Muslims. The Byzantine leadership had noted the earlier Muslim successes, but they did not regard them as especially important. The empire was huge, and Byzantine rulers were well used to raids and attacks from outsiders. The capture of Damascus, however, marked a turning point and revealed the Muslim armies to be a genuine threat.

Heraclius, residing in the Syrian city of Antioch, began assembling an army to destroy the Muslim invaders. Historians disagree about the size of the army, but it likely numbered in the tens of thousands. These were disciplined, veteran soldiers, including a division of Syrian Arab cavalry. However, several accounts show the army was internally divided. For one thing, it was composed of Greeks, Armenians, and Arabs. They all spoke different languages and regarded the type of Christianity practiced by the others with contempt. In addition, some of the soldiers were used to fighting in mountainous regions rather than in the flatter, fertile areas through which they then marched.

Outnumbered, the Muslim armies quickly withdrew, surrendering the cities that they had so recently conquered. By spring 636, the Muslim armies had retreated back into Arabia, where they sent urgent calls for reinforcements. Umar realized the importance of this challenge. A display of weakness at that point could unravel the loyalty of the Bedouin tribes and destroy the fledgling Muslim state. Umar sent messengers throughout Arabia. He ordered all able-bodied Muslim men to join the Muslim army and prepare for the great battle to come.

By mid-summer 636, the Muslim army numbered about twenty thousand men. The force, commanded by Khalid, included veterans of all the previous battles. As he considered the men in his ranks, Khalid pulled the most senior soldiers out of the line. These were members of the original Muslim community who had known the Prophet personally. They had memorized whole sections of the Quran, as well as numerous stories about Muhammad. If the Muslim army were destroyed in the upcoming battle, Khalid did not want the Muslim tradition to disappear.

The Muslim and Byzantine armies approached each other near the Yarmuk River in modern-day Jordan. "This is one of God's battles," Khalid told his soldiers. "There should be neither pride nor wrongdoing in it. Strive sincerely, seeking God in your work." The Muslim soldiers were brave and motivated. Some sources say they chanted religious verses as they approached the Byzantine positions.

Accounts of the battle are not clear. Some writers describe the Byzantines pushing the Muslims back to their camps. Among the tents, the Muslim soldiers were apparently shamed by the appearance of women, urging them to resist and in some cases even joining the fight.

The Muslims took heart and counterattacked. They caught the Byzantines off balance and prevented them from coordinating an effective defense. The Muslim cavalry commander noticed that the Byzantine cavalry and infantry had become separated. He ordered his cavalry to ride between the two forces, which enabled the mounted soldiers to slaughter isolated Byzantine infantry. At this point, sensing the battle was swinging toward the Arab Muslims, the Christian Arab tribes fled or, in some versions of the story, went over to the other side.

Further spreading confusion in the Byzantine ranks was a dust storm that reportedly covered the battlefield and prevented Byzantine units from supporting each other. The Muslims attacked and stormed the main Byzantine camps. Discipline among the Byzantine units began to break down as news spread that the Christian Arab tribes had defected.

The Muslims captured a bridge over the Yarmuk, trapping the Byzantine army between two bluffs. The Muslims then drove the Byzantines into a maze of deep, dry gullies and hunted them down. The remaining Byzantine army, along with its commanders, was destroyed. Even the emperor's brother, Theodorus, was killed. A chronicler later remembered the Battle of Yarmuk as "the first and fearful and incurable fall of the Roman army."

When Heraclius heard the news of the defeat, he knew he had few options. He had no large force capable of resisting the Muslim onslaught. The Muslim army could march straight into the heart of the empire. To counter this threat, he ordered all Byzantine forces in Syria to assemble and withdraw to a new line of defense in the mountainous region of southern Anatolia (in modern-day Turkey). "Farewell, O Syria," the emperor said, "and what an excellent country this is for the enemy."

SYRIA IS CONQUERED

The Muslim armies moved speedily to exploit their stunning victory. Most Syrian cities, including Antioch, where Heraclius himself had established a residence, fell quickly. Some Syrian towns welcomed the invaders, or at least, hoping to escape brutal treatment, tried to put them in a good mood as they approached. At the town of Shayzar, local leaders gave the Muslims a welcome usually reserved for important guests. They greeted the soldiers with music played on drums and cymbals.

Other cities tried to hold out. At Homs, the city authorities argued they should at least resist the Muslims until winter. They assumed that the Arab soldiers, clad only in sandals, would be unable to endure the cold. But when the Muslim army was still there the next spring, the city surrendered.

Homs and other cities had little choice but to accept the terms offered by the Muslim generals, who used the Quran as a guide in treating the city's populations. One verse urges Muslims to "kill the idolators wherever you find them." But it also orders Muslims to be generous: "If they repent, pray regularly, and give the alms tax, then let them go their way, for God is forgiving and merciful."

The people of Syria and Palestine were mostly Christian and Jewish. The Muslims did not force them to convert but relegated them to the status of *dhimmi*, meaning "protected." Under this arrangement, the Jews and Christians could keep their property. But they could not form an army of any kind. They had to pay a special tax to the Muslims. This tax took many forms. In at least one case, a town simply handed over a quantity of wheat and olive oil to the Muslims. Paying the tax was considered a mark of lowly status. The Arabs said that "he who acknowledges a tax acknowledges humiliation."

As Muhammad had ordered, the Muslims did not openly attempt to convert Christians and Jews to Islam. The Quran, after all, acknowledged that Jews, Christians, and Muslims all worshipped the same god, although in different ways: "Will you dispute with us about God? When he is our lord and he is your lord! We have our words and you have your words but we are sincerely his." In addition, the Muslims understood that a peaceful, content population would also regularly pay taxes, providing Muslim rulers with an invaluable and steady stream of wealth. In many cases, conquered and conqueror coexisted peacefully.

The Muslims respected Christian churches. But since they needed structures for their religious services, they sometimes took a portion of a local church to use as a mosque. At Homs, the Muslims took one-fourth of the church. In Damascus, they used half the cathedral (a church that is a regional center of authority).

SHARING SPACE

Modern archaeological discoveries show that Muslims and Christians shared places of worship after the Muslim conquest. In a small Syrian town in Negev Subeita, a Byzantine-era church has a mihrab in its foundation. A mihrab is a door-sized impression built into the wall of every mosque. It points Muslim worshippers in the direction of Mecca, toward which they pray.

When Muslim forces encountered more resistance—as happened along the coast of the Mediterranean Sea—they were less forgiving. In the coastal cities, the inhabitants identified more strongly with the Byzantines. They could also be reinforced from the sea. In this era, armies often used a tactic called a siege. They surrounded an enemy city and prevented food and other goods from entering, in this way attempting to starve the inhabitants into surrender. But supplied by ships and protected by stout walls, the city of Caesarea held off a Muslim siege for several years. Finally, the Muslims stormed and conquered the city. Because the city had been hostile, Muslim soldiers enslaved most of the inhabitants and sent them to Arabia.

After the Muslim conquests, Syria would never be the same. The Greek-speaking rulers, who had always looked west to the Byzantine, Greek, and Roman empires, were replaced. The new rulers were Muslims who spoke Arabic. They oriented themselves south toward Medina and Mecca.

PEOPLE OF THE BOOK

The Muslim perception of Judaism and Christianity is complex. While Islam insists on being a true revelation (the word of God), it also reveres the Jewish patriarch Abraham as the father of religions, and Jesus as a great prophet second only to Muhammad. Muslims also acknowledge that God revealed himself to Jews and Christians prior to revealing himself to Muhammad.

Jews from Damascus consult an elder, who tells them that Muhammad was a prophet truly sent from God. This image comes from a Turkish manuscript from the 1600s.

JERUSALEM FALLS

The only city in the region that still held out was the ancient city of Jerusalem—which was sacred to Jews, Christians, and Muslims. Sophronius, who had earlier hoped to see the Muslims' "destruction and complete ruin," realized that he could not resist for long. In a bid for time, Sophronius offered to surrender—but only to Umar himself.

Umar made the journey to Jerusalem in the winter of 637–638. As he neared the Muslim army camp, his senior generals greeted him. Umar was dressed in a tattered cloak that he had faithfully repaired and worn for several years. When he saw his army commanders dressed in luxurious Syrian cloth, he spoke sharply: "Do you come to me dressed like that? Have you changed so much in two years? You all deserve to be dismissed in disgrace!" The generals pulled aside their rich clothes to reveal the armor underneath, battered and dented after dozens of battles. Umar, however, was not impressed.

Umar later received a Christian delegation from Jerusalem and agreed to terms for the city's peaceful surrender. He approached the city gates on a white camel, barefoot, and wearing the white linen of a religious pilgrim. Sophronius, who was dressed in black and kept his disdain for Muslims to himself, was there to meet him. Control of one of the world's holiest cities passed to Islam.

Sophronius accompanied the barefoot caliph through the city. He showed Umar the Holy Sepulchre, a church built over the site where Christ was reportedly buried. Outside, the Muslim call to prayer sounded. Umar left the building and unrolled a prayer rug on the porch, later explaining that

Sophronius (far right) *and Umar* (second from right) *tour Jerusalem after its surrender. This 1415 French painting shows Umar visiting the old Jewish temple, which had been destroyed by the Romans. Tradition holds that Umar and his soldiers cleared the site out of respect. He later had a mosque built at one end of the area.*

had he prayed in the church, it would have to have been converted into a mosque. Later, Muslims built a mosque on the site of the porch, leaving the church intact.

At the end of the tour, Umar visited the Sakhra Rock, where Jewish patriarch Abraham supposedly prepared his son Isaac for sacrifice and where Muhammad, on a

Both Jews and Muslims consider the Sakhra Rock to be a holy site. The rock lies at the center of the Dome of the Rock.

journey with the angel Gabriel, had ascended to heaven. In 695 Muslims built the Dome of the Rock on this site. In modern times, it is the most holy place in Islam, after Mecca and Medina.

ESTABLISHING AN EMPIRE

Umar had become the ruler of most of the Middle East, including numerous Christian and Jewish communities. In a series of decisions, he consolidated the conquered regions and established a system to maintain his empire. This system was based on "Umar's Principles."

Umar's first principle was to keep the Muslim army, made up of men from the Arab tribes, apart from the local cities and population. He did not allow Muslim soldiers to settle or farm land among the conquered peoples. The intent was to keep the Muslim army distinct, firm in its Islamic faith, and mobile. In addition, Umar wanted to keep the soldiers dependent on Medina—not on conquered towns—for support and money.

Umar's second principle was that conquered territory would be collectively owned by the Muslim people. It would be maintained in common to support the Muslim armies and the vulnerable of the community—widows, orphans, and the poor. Because of this decree, conquered territories were not divided up into separate estates for generals and soldiers, as was common in other parts of the world. Umar had no intention of allowing Arab Muslims to create a ruling class that was tied to individual pieces of land. Instead, using taxation, he funneled wealth from the conquered territories into a central treasury. That money was then distributed to the community.

"THEIR KINGDOM WAS A DREAM"

As the Muslim armies were fighting and advancing in Syria, Muslim forces also marched to attack the other great empire of the day, the Persian Empire. The empire was ruled by a warrior class made up of noble families. Members of this class mostly followed Zoroastrianism, a religion based on the belief that the world is the battleground between a good god and an evil god. The Zoroastrians worshipped fire, which they considered to be a sacred element. Priests tended fires in small temples under domed roofs. The majority of Persians, especially those who were not in the ruling class, did not follow Zoroastrianism. They were mostly Christian.

The empire was recovering from its disastrous war with
the Byzantine Empire, which had ended in defeat and chaos.
After the war, the Persians were unable to restore their order
or prestige. A number of emperors succeeded to the throne
in the late 620s. Each emperor ruled for less than a year,
heightening a general sense of instability.

By 632, the year Muhammad died, Muslim forces were
already probing the weakly defended border along Persia.
In the next year, a Muslim army under Khalid conquered
several towns on the Euphrates River, just inside Persian
territory. These towns surrendered quickly and agreed to send
tribute to Medina. These attacks, however, did not draw the
full attention of the Persian army.

In 634 a small Muslim army finally met the Persian army
at the Battle of the Bridge. The Muslims attacked across wet
farmland, which bogged down their cavalry. Worse for the
Muslims, the Persian army included soldiers riding elephants.
One elephant supposedly trampled the Muslim commander
to death. The Muslim army withdrew in disorder after losing
a third of its men.

This setback was not discouraging to the Muslims
because of the spectacular victories being reported from
Syria. Umar, however, did not forget the defeat. Within
three years, he had raised another army and sent it north to
invade Persia. The commander was a general named Saad.
Sometime between 636 and 638 (historians are unsure), the
Persian army confronted this force.

The forces clashed in the Battle of Qadisiya. Both
armies were well led, and the soldiers battled for several
days in bitter fighting. The Muslims avoided their earlier

mistake of being drawn into wet land, remaining instead on the edge of the desert. The combat was done mostly on foot, between men with swords. But Muslim archers also took part in the battle, and their equipment was superior to that of the Persians. One Persian soldier, who later converted to Islam, described the difference in the forces: "One of our archers would shoot an arrow from his bow but it would do no more than attach itself to the garment of an Arab whereas their arrow would tear through a coat of mail and the double cuirass [metal armor] we had on." The Persian army was eventually defeated and its commander killed.

Mesopotamia was left open to the invaders. This ancient land, which straddled the Tigris and Euphrates rivers, was one

QADISIYA

The Battle of Qadisiya is remembered in the Muslim world as a moment when a small Muslim force overcame the mighty Persian army. Saddam Hussein, who ruled the modern Muslim nation of Iraq from 1979 to 2003, mentioned the battle repeatedly in his political speeches. In 2003, when U.S.-led forces invaded Iraq, the Iraqi media described the war as Hussein's Qadisiya. With this reference, Hussein hoped to inspire the ill-equipped Iraqi forces to resist and defeat the powerful U.S. military. But U.S. forces were too strong. The Iraqi army quickly crumbled and disbanded after the initial attack.

of the most famous and rich areas in the world. The Muslim soldiers soon approached the capital city of Ctesiphon, where the emperor's palace was defended by strong earthworks. The Muslim forces, unwilling to risk a major assault, laid siege to the palace. Within a few days, the discouraged Persian defenders withdrew.

Inside the palace walls, the Muslims discovered a magnificent hall, which they later converted into a mosque. Muslim soldiers also discovered the emperor's treasure, which they added to an extraordinary haul of booty. The Muslims then rode their horses through the swift Tigris River and invaded the main part of the city.

Much of the empire to the west, however, remained unconquered. The Persian emperor, Hurmuzan, retreated

Persians built the arch at Ctesiphon around 400. During the 500s, a Persian king incorporated the arch into his palace, making it into the roof of a banquet hall.

into this region to organize more resistance to the Muslim onslaught. He decided to make his stand in the city of Susa, which was well protected by a castle and a river. Accounts say that the city was able to hold out for two years before its defenses were broken. The Muslims captured Hurmuzan and took him back to Medina to face Umar.

Their meeting contains an interesting story. After some brief conversation, Umar told Hurmuzan that he would be executed in revenge for the Muslim deaths his resistance had caused. Hurmuzan asked for a drink of water. When he received it, Hurmuzan said he was afraid that Umar would kill him before he could drink his water. Umar assured him that he would be allowed to finish the water before his execution. Hurmuzan raised the cup and spilled the water. When Umar again threatened Hurmuzan with death, Hurmuzan coolly replied that Umar could not kill him. As Hurmuzan explained, he had never finished drinking the water, and Umar had promised he would not be killed before he did. Umar was reportedly furious at this ploy, but he had given his word. Later, Hurmuzan converted to Islam and lived the rest of his life in Medina.

With the victories at Qadisiya and Yarmuk, the territory under Muslim rule encompassed much of the Middle East. Two great and ancient empires had been shocked by the upstart religion. As one Arab poet wrote, "O men, do you not see how Persia has been ruined and its inhabitants humiliated? They have become slaves who pasture your sheep, as if their kingdom was a dream."

CHAPTER FIVE
THE CONQUEST OF EGYPT

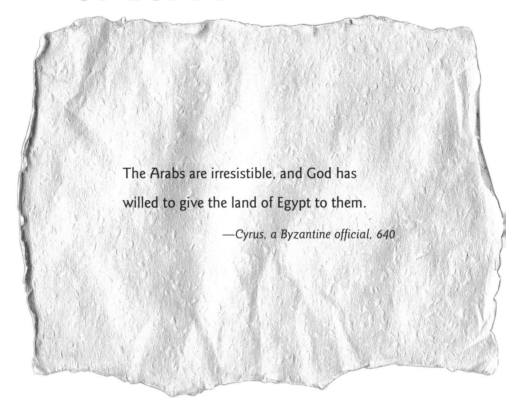

The Arabs are irresistible, and God has
willed to give the land of Egypt to them.

—*Cyrus, a Byzantine official, 640*

Muslim attention swung to Egypt, a rich and ancient civilization and a province of the Byzantine Empire. Egyptian territory followed the course of the Nile River from north to south, a band of green vegetation nourished by the river's waters. By the A.D. 600s, Egypt's ancient glory had faded. The famous Egyptian pyramids were already thousands of years old.

Egypt had long contended with raids from Bedouin

tribesmen. Walled cities and outposts protected the country. The capital city was Alexandria, which lies on the coast of the Mediterranean Sea and hosted a garrison of at least twenty-five thousand soldiers.

Egypt was not as strong as it appeared, however. The dominant religion was Christianity, but this faith brought more strife than unity. The version of Christianity practiced by the majority of Egyptians—by people called Copts— clashed directly with the Christianity supported by the Byzantine Empire. As a result, many Egyptians regarded Byzantine officials with suspicion and hostility. Moreover, Egypt was still recovering from a plague and war. The plague had swept through the region in the mid-500s, possibly killing more than one-third of Egypt's inhabitants. In the early 600s, the area had been occupied by the Persians, who conquered Alexandria and sacked the monasteries (religious complexes) in the surrounding countryside.

After eleven years of Persian rule, the Byzantines again assumed control of the land. This change resulted in no peace, however. When a Byzantine official named Cyrus arrived in Alexandria to assume his position as head of the city, the local Coptic Christian leader ordered the Egyptian clergy to resist. All attempts to heal the divide between the Christian groups failed. Cyrus attempted to crush Coptic resistance by having Coptic leaders arrested, and sometimes tortured and executed. Thus the Arab Muslim forces approached an Egypt that was internally divided.

Following the defeat at Yarmuk, Cyrus had negotiated a truce with Umar. The Egyptians paid the Arabs a heavy tax to avoid attack by the victorious Muslim armies. The

This mosaic, made in Jordan around 550, shows the tall walls that surrounded the city of Alexandria, Egypt. The Greek general Alexander the Great founded Alexandria in 331 B.C.

Egyptian leaders followed the familiar tactic of stalling for time. They knew that any number of situations—a defeat, a revolt, a destabilizing death of a leader, or some internal squabble over power—could cause the Muslim army to retreat. By 640, however, the Muslim armies were stronger than ever and preparing to invade Egypt. Historians are unsure exactly why. The truce between the Egyptians and the Arabs may have expired. Cyrus had left Alexandria, and Emperor Heraclius may have replaced him with a leader who was less inclined to pay tribute and more inclined to fight.

In 640 Amr ibn al-As, who had already won fame in the Syrian campaigns, led thirteen thousand men across the desert and into Egyptian territory. They approached a Byzantine garrison at the Egyptian city of Babylon. A Byzantine army approached from Alexandria. Amr defeated this force by sending a detachment of cavalry around the Byzantine army at night. When the battle was joined the next day, these horsemen burst out of the hills behind the Byzantine force, throwing it into confusion. The Byzantine army suffered serious losses as it retreated.

Amr then laid siege to Babylon, but the city was powerful and well defended. As the siege wore on, however, the defenders began to lose hope. They received no relief from other Byzantine forces. The leaders of Babylon offered to surrender the city if Amr guaranteed them safe passage to Alexandria with their gold. Amr agreed to these terms. Babylon, the most important city in Egypt except for Alexandria, fell into Muslim hands.

By then Heraclius had died. His death caused upheaval in the Byzantine Empire as various successors engaged in murderous competition to ascend to the throne. In this environment, Egypt received little attention. The Muslim army was able to leave Babylon and advance north to Alexandria, the magnificent and well-defended capital of the country.

FROM ALEXANDRIA TO POINTS EAST

The Muslim forces settled into a siege. As at Babylon, the Muslims were not expert in this form of warfare. The city also had access to the sea. Ships carrying food and reinforcements could easily sail into the city's harbor—so the defenders would not surrender because of hunger.

Unable to storm the walls, the Muslims withdrew and reconsidered their tactics. Meanwhile, Cyrus was restored as ruler of Egypt. Soon after he returned to Alexandria, he began secret negotiations to surrender the city and the country to Amr. Cyrus and Amr soon reached an agreement. The two forces would observe a truce for one year, allowing time for the Byzantine soldiers and officials to leave Alexandria. Then the Byzantines would open the city gates to the Arab army, transferring power peacefully. When Cyrus announced the deal, his officers were shocked. According to legend, Cyrus explained that "the Arabs are irresistible, and God has willed to give the land of Egypt to them."

Cyrus is a fascinating and mysterious figure. He has been portrayed as a coward—a schemer who surrendered Alexandria against the wishes of his men, the townspeople, and the emperor. Historians puzzle over his actions, especially his decision not to resist the Muslim invaders. On the other hand, he has been described as a realist who displayed a measure of wisdom. The Muslims had already seized much of the Middle East. Cyrus recognized this reality and was able to spare Alexandria the horror of a drawn-out siege and a bitter fight that might end in a massacre.

When he reportedly told the people of Alexandria that they had been surrendered, they were enraged and threatened to stone him to death. With tears running down his cheeks, Cyrus explained that it was the only way to save Alexandria's women and children. The townspeople relented, but Cyrus did not live another year. He was supposedly broken down by his failure to protect Egypt. One story says that in his despair, he sickened and died before Muslim forces entered the city. In another account, he committed suicide by sipping poison hidden in his ring.

Another mystery surrounding the fall of Alexandria is the role of the Coptic Church. Some historians say that the Copts actively helped the Muslim forces, since Muslim rule was more attractive than the oppression experienced under the Byzantines. Other historians argue that the Copts resisted the invaders vigorously, despite their own misgivings about living under Byzantine rule.

THE GLORY THAT WAS ALEXANDRIA

Alexandria was founded in 331 B.C. by the Greek general Alexander the Great. By the time Amr approached its walls, the city was almost one thousand years old. It was home to more than one million people and was one of the most sophisticated and beautiful cities in the world. Alexandria sits on the Mediterranean Sea. Its famous lighthouse towered several hundred feet above the water, guiding ships safely into the harbor. Its library held a priceless collection of books and manuscripts. The Muslim conquerors were awed by Alexandria. One concluded, "I have made the Pilgrimage to Mecca sixty times, but if Allah had suffered me to stay a month at Alexandria . . . that month would be dearer to me."

The true story about Egypt's conquest may never be known. What is certain is that the Byzantine garrison withdrew from Alexandria, along with most of the Byzantine elites, in the months after Cyrus and Amr concluded their agreement. At the end of the year, the gates of the city were opened, and Amr rode into Alexandria on a white horse, followed by six thousand cavalry. The ancient city of one million people was under the control of the Arab Muslims.

Amr sent a message to Umar: "I have taken a city of which I can only say that it contains 4,000 palaces, 4,000 baths, 400 theaters, 1,200 green grocers, and 40,000 Jews." The city included a towering lighthouse that was regarded as one of the seven wonders of the world. The conquerors would build many mosques in the city, including one in the lighthouse. Almost one thousand years of Greek-speaking rule in Alexandria was ended.

Amr followed the pattern set by other conquering Arab armies. He withdrew his army from the temptations and distractions of Alexandria and returned to a campsite outside Babylon. Amr's old tent still stood, and on its site

This artist's interpretation of the lighthouse of Alexandria was painted in the 1800s.

was constructed a mosque. A city called Cairo—the capital of modern Egypt—eventually grew up around the site.

Amr spent much of the next year wiping out isolated Egyptian towns that refused to accept Muslim rule. With this campaign finished, Amr looked westward. In a series of strikes, he captured ancient cities strung along North Africa's Mediterranean coast. Tripoli, Sabratha, and Leptis Magna (all in modern-day Libya) fell to Amr's army.

Not content with this success, Amr turned south. He sent his soldiers into desert regions where few conquerors had ever dared to venture. As a result, Islam penetrated deep into North Africa. Various oases complexes became Muslim outposts.

As these successful campaigns continued, Amr returned to Egypt, his men rich with weapons, armor, jewels, gold, and slaves. Stories of Amr's wealth and ostentatious living eventually reached Umar. His reaction was predictable. "I have had enough experience of dishonest officials and my suspicion has been aroused against you," Umar wrote to Amr. Umar ordered Amr to send some of his wealth back to Medina. In 645 Umar went further. He removed Amr from the governorship of Egypt and ordered him to return to Medina.

Egypt began to slowly transform from a Byzantine province into an Islamic region. The nation's bounty of grain, once sent to the cities of the Mediterranean, was instead sent to Medina and Mecca. The majority of the population at first was Christian, but over the centuries, the Arab and Muslim presence grew. Eventually, Egypt became a center of Islamic commerce and culture, although the Coptic Christian minority remained.

CLASH OF CULTURES

A story of the siege of Alexandria in 642 has come down to historians, giving us some tantalizing details about how Muslims and Alexandrians saw each other at that time. According to this story, a young Egyptian boy and the grown son of a wealthy Byzantine became curious about the Arab forces outside the city. The man suggested to the young boy that they "take a look at these Arabs who are fighting us." The Byzantine dressed for the expedition in a fine robe, a gold headband, and a decorated sword. His horse was strong and healthy. The boy followed on a small pony. Once they had left the city's walls, the two rode up to a small hill that overlooked a Bedouin tent. Nearby, a horse was tied to a spear that had been thrust into the ground. The Byzantine and the boy marveled at how the Arabs seemed to have very little equipment but had accomplished so much. Suddenly, an Arab man came out of the tent and saw them. The Byzantine seemed unconcerned, and he continued to talk to the boy as the Arab grabbed his spear and mounted his horse. When the Arab started galloping toward them, the Byzantine and his friend fled. The Arab caught up with the Byzantine, spearing him to death. The boy made it back safely within the city walls. When he looked back, the Arab was walking back to his tent. Ignoring the Byzantine's rich items and horse, he stuck the spear back into the sandy earth, tied up his horse, and returned to his tent without telling anyone. Decades after this incident, the young boy (by then an elderly man) told his story to the Muslim governor of Egypt. The old man said that the Arab had been short and thin—like a "human swordfish."

We cannot be certain this event ever took place. Nonetheless, this small story conceals an enormous amount of information. The Byzantine is depicted as wealthy and frivolous, someone who knows little of danger. The Arab, on the other hand, is quick to fight. More important, he is not interested in the goods of this world. He does not plunder the corpse, and neither does he boast to anyone of his exploits. This is how the Arabs saw themselves—as virtuous and tough soldiers fighting a pompous and wealthy but also weak and soft enemy.

Arab horsemen ride to battle with banners and trumpets. This painting was made in Iran in the 1200s.

UMAR'S INITIATIVES

At the head of what had suddenly become an empire—a political power with vast territories—Umar had to create a system to deal with the annual inflows of tribute. Umar at first distributed the entire surplus to tribal chiefs. He then created a more orderly system by paying yearly salaries. The Prophet's former companions, Muhammad's former wives, and those who had performed extraordinary military service received the largest share. A soldier's salary depended on the battles he had fought in or how long he had been a Muslim. An individual's current position in society, whether rich or poor, carried little weight in these considerations. For example, a poor man who had been one of Muhammad's earliest followers would receive more than a powerful chief who had converted later. Umar distributed all the money that came into the Medina treasury. He refused to create any kind of reserve to help cope with famine or disease, declaring, "We trust in God and his Prophet, they are our reserves."

To keep track of when people converted to Islam, Umar decided to establish a calendar. It was Umar who set the date 622—the year Muhammad fled Mecca and settled in Medina—as the first year of the Islamic calendar.

Along with his salary system and calendar, Umar insisted that no Muslim man could have more than four wives (based on the Quran's teaching that no man could realistically afford more than the four individual houses necessary to shelter them). In addition, Umar insisted that no house be larger than Muhammad's modest dwelling in Medina.

Umar could be brusque and severe. He rebuked his commanders if they ever appeared to forget his authority.

MARGIN OF ERROR

Umar's Islamic calendar was out of step with modern calendars. It followed the cycles of the moon (most modern calendars are solar—based on the sun). Because a lunar (moon) month is shorter than a solar month, the lunar year slips behind the solar year by a few days every cycle. Because of this difference, modern historians are uncertain exactly when the events of Muhammad's life took place, or when the great battles of the Islamic conquest were fought. One historian said there is a two- to four-year margin of error in the dates for most major events in early Arab Muslim history.

Aisha, Muhammad's widow, remarked, "When he spoke, he made one hear; when he walked, he was brisk; and when he struck, he hurt." But Umar was also humble. He once stressed to a full mosque that he was "but an ordinary person like you." In Medina people would stop him on the street to ask his opinion or ask him to settle small disputes, such as a quarrel over a cow. He always took these matters seriously, no matter how insignificant. When Umar's own son appeared drunk in public, Umar insisted that he be punished to the full extent of the law—just like any other Muslim. The son was whipped eighty times, which killed him.

When Umar was sixty-three, an enraged slave from Persia attacked him. He stabbed Umar several times before killing himself. Umar, the second caliph, was dead. His achievements, however, had been immense. He had overseen

Islam's expansion and established the necessary structure and codes to rule the new empire. Umar was buried under the floor of Aisha's bedroom—next to the Prophet and Abu Bakr. His head faced Mecca.

Umar lies dying in the arms of fellow companions Ali and Uthman as guards carry away the man who stabbed him. A Turkish artist painted this miniature around 1600.

CHOOSING THE THIRD CALIPH

Umar, like Abu Bakr before him, had already planned for a succession to his rule. Unlike Abu Bakr, however, Umar did not make the choice. He called for a meeting of the companions and other high-ranking members of the community to select the next caliph.

After some deliberation, the group settled on two candidates—Ali and an elderly man named Uthman. Uthman was in many ways an unremarkable trader. He had almost no leadership experience. But that, as it turned out, was what many in the community desired. Uthman was seen as the safe choice, someone who would not inspire any radical changes.

Ali, on the other hand, while known for his piety and fierceness in battle, gave little clue as to how exactly he would rule were he made caliph. When asked whether he would follow the example set by the other two caliphs, Ali answered no. He would rule as he, in accordance with God, saw fit. This answer did not comfort Ali's opponents. In the end, they selected the seventy-year-old Uthman as the third caliph.

CHAPTER SIX
THE TRAGEDY OF UTHMAN

> You have departed from the ways of the
> Holy Prophet. You are amassing wealth,
> you have raised your palatial buildings and
> have become the victims of luxury!
>
> —*Abu Dharr al-Ghafari, one of*
> *Muhammad's first companions, circa 651*

In contrast to Umar's scowl and severity, Uthman had a gentle demeanor. When addressing the faithful in the mosque after his elevation to caliph, he paused in mid-speech and apologized to his listeners because the moment had overwhelmed him. Uthman had been one of Muhammad's trusted companions. He married one of Muhammad's daughters and, after she died, married another. Muhammad supposedly described Uthman as modest and shy. A wealthy merchant with an established family, Uthman was among the first half-dozen converts to Islam.

Uthman was known for his kindness, his generosity, and his business sense. He bought food for the Medina community during a period of famine and regularly sent supplies to Muslim armies. However, Uthman was not a

This Indian painting from the late 1700s shows Uthman praying with his Quran and prayer beads.

warrior. He had avoided almost all the battles of early Islam. In the middle of one fight, he had abruptly fled, an act for which Muhammad had forgiven him.

Ali and his clan, however, would never forgive Uthman for denying what they saw as Ali's rightful place at the head of the Muslim community. The appointments of Abu Bakr and Umar had been difficult to endure, but Ali's followers could not deny that Abu Bakr and Umar were wise, strong, and respected leaders. Uthman, however, was uninspiring. Worse, he came from the Umayadds, an old clan—part of the Quraysh tribe—that had ruled Mecca before Muhammad had prevailed over the city. To Ali's supporters, Uthman's appointment was like a restoration of Mecca's pre-Islamic rulers. Over time, this bitterness would grow, harden, and burst into violence.

UTHMAN THE CALIPH

Uthman's reign began well. He demonstrated his administrative skill, knitting the vast Arab Islamic empire more closely and efficiently together. He gathered together a group of financial administrators who kept a close eye on tax revenue. While this work may seem dull compared to the conquests of Umar's reign, Uthman's changes had an impact on the collection of money—and money is never dull. Uthman increased annual payments to soldiers, widows of soldiers slain in battle, and members of the original Muslim community. He gave awards to the parents of all Arab boys born in garrison towns. Soon the central Muslim authority was paying out and keeping track of one hundred thousand salaries annually.

Uthman relaxed some of Umar's strict decrees. Umar had insisted that no man's house could exceed the dimensions of Muhammad's dwelling. Uthman himself built a magnificent palace in Medina. Many of the first converts to Islam built their own palaces in major cities across the Middle East. Umar had restricted the movement of Muhammad's companions. They were not allowed to leave Medina without his permission. Under Uthman, many companions did move and resettle—especially in the newly conquered regions of Syria. There, they lived in relative luxury, sustained by their conquests and taxes. This situation was in direct contrast to Umar's belief that Muslims should be a "poor, highly mobile army of faith."

In addition to enjoying the fruits of the empire, Uthman was forced to protect it. When news of Umar's death spread, captive nations revolted. In Persia, local rebellions occurred

THE FIVE PILLARS OF ISLAM

In its first one hundred years, Islam matured from a tiny band of followers in a remote town to become an empire stretching across the world. Over time, rules and beliefs that formed the religion's foundation became known as the Five Pillars of Islam. They summarize the beliefs of faithful Muslims. The Five Pillars are:

- **Faith:** Each Muslim professes that Allah is the only God and that Muhammad is his messenger.

- **Prayer:** Each Muslim is to pray five times a day in the direction of Mecca.

- **Alms:** Each Muslim is to give charity to the poor.

- **Fasting:** Each Muslim is to fast during the holy month of Ramadan.

- **Pilgrimage:** Each Muslim is to make a pilgrimage to Mecca, if possible.

constantly, confronting Muslim armies stationed at Kufa and Basra. Former provinces of the Persian Empire in modern-day Armenia, Azerbaijan, and other areas quickly reestablished independence. They repulsed Muslim armies for five years (and destroyed two Muslim armies in the process) before the Muslims reasserted control.

In 644 Egypt revolted, supported by a Byzantine fleet of three hundred ships that had arrived in Alexandria's harbor. Citizens and Byzantine soldiers massacred Alexandria's one-thousand-man Muslim garrison. A Byzantine army commanded by a general named Manuel reoccupied the area around the city.

To restore Muslim control, Uthman appointed Amr to lead a force. Showing the same cunning that had delivered Egypt into his hands earlier, Amr lured the Byzantine army south. He fought the Byzantines to a standstill and then drove them back into Alexandria, where they took shelter behind the city walls. Through either a betrayal or an assault, Amr was able to seize a strategic gateway in the wall and thus enter the city.

Alexandria was again under Muslim control. This time, however, Amr let his troops take revenge upon the citizens who had risen up in support of the Byzantines. The soldiers either slaughtered or enslaved the rebels. Amr, intending never to allow the city to be used again as a base for the Byzantines, destroyed the walls that faced east—the direction from which a Muslim army would approach the city.

WRITING DOWN THE QURAN

Uthman was also responsible for the first edited, authoritative, written version of the Quran. Until then, the Quran had mostly been recited. Members of the Qurra (Quran readers) traveled around the empire, teaching the verses to others. Only a few passages, mostly dealing with legal questions, had been written down.

Through the process of oral recitation and teaching, slightly altered versions of the verses emerged in different parts of the empire. Uthman was determined to eradicate these differences and ensure that the community used only a single Quran.

He appointed a group that included several men who had known Muhammad personally. They painstakingly combed Medina and Mecca for written verses and variations in oral verses. When the project was complete, the Quran consisted of 77,000 words and 6,211 verses, which were divided into 112 *suras*—Arabic for "row"—or chapters.

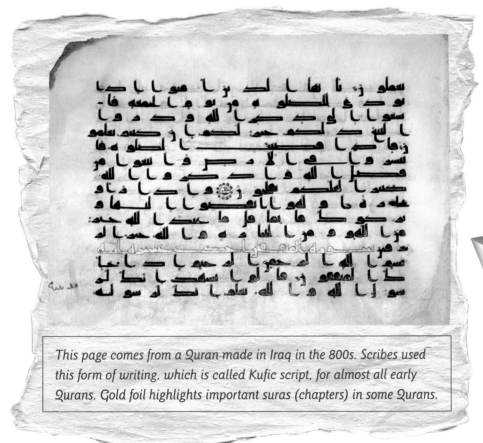

This page comes from a Quran made in Iraq in the 800s. Scribes used this form of writing, which is called Kufic script, for almost all early Qurans. Gold foil highlights important suras (chapters) in some Qurans.

The suras were placed into the Quran according to their length, with the longest first and the shortest last. In Muslim eyes, the order of the suras makes little difference, since all words from God hold equal value.

According to tradition, Uthman sent four copies of the Quran to the four corners of the empire—where they became the sources for all copies of the Quran since then. None of these originals has survived.

Early Islamic tradition banned realistic paintings of religious figures. Over time, the ban relaxed. Skilled calligraphers began to make images out of the words of the Quran. The lines of this bird, from an Iranian work of the late 1600s, spell out (in script) "In the Name of the Almighty."

LEARNING THE QURAN

Young Muslims learn the Quran by first memorizing verses and short suras. As the students learn more passages, the Quran becomes a cohesive whole—even though it is not presented in chronological order. The life of the Hebrew prophet Moses, for example, is recounted in forty-four separate suras. Devout Muslims learn all these references. For them, a single verse can evoke an entire story, an entire world.

When non-Muslims approach the Quran, they often draw back in confusion—partly because they are reading the book in translation. Muslims have never approved of translations of the Quran. They argue that the book can be truly understood and appreciated only in the original Arabic—the very words of God. The beauty of the poetry, they say, is literally untranslatable. In addition, non-Muslims (especially Europeans and North Americans) typically read the text with the expectation of a beginning, a middle, and an end. But the Quran is organized strictly by the length of the suras. Chronology is no factor.

REBELLION AGAINST UTHMAN

Uthman's first six years as caliph were successful and prosperous. In 651, however, Uthman was leaning over a well that had recently been repaired. As he was pointing out a stone that needed further work, a ring slipped off his finger and disappeared into the well. This was not an ordinary ring. It was one of the few artifacts that Muhammad himself had used. Since then, each caliph had worn the ring as an emblem of his position. Although workers dug up the mud at the bottom of the well and sifted through it handful by handful, they never found the ring. The Muslim community considered this loss a terrible omen. Later, this incident would be used to describe the two eras of Uthman's reign—the first marked by glory and prosperity, the second by strife and bitterness.

About the time of the lost ring, Uthman's authority began to crumble—and many say that Uthman himself deserved much of the blame. Whereas Umar had ruthlessly maintained discipline over the Arab Muslim rulers, Uthman began relying on his family members to keep control. But many of these family members were incompetent. When their incompetence became public, Uthman pardoned their offenses. This treatment was in direct contrast with Umar, who spared no one and even had his own son flogged as punishment.

Under Uthman, his Umayadd clan gained enormous wealth and power. The Umayadd ruled all the top cities and held all the top government posts. Uthman further strengthened his rule by marrying off his daughters to powerful men—all of them in the Umayadd clan. Those outside the clan were shut out completely.

Other Arab clans grew resentful, restive, and then enraged. The positions of power in the Islamic state appeared to be falling under the hereditary rule of Uthman's family and kinsmen. Making the resentment worse, many of the officeholders had been late and reluctant converts to Islam.

More signs of disquiet appeared. Those who remembered the Prophet and the first caliphs' frugality and simple lives recoiled from the lifestyles of Uthman and his clan. When Abu Bakr had been caliph, he occasionally milked a cow by himself. Umar had worn the same clothes for years, patching and sewing them when they ripped.

These examples seemed to be forgotten. The new Arab lords lived in palaces, with their every whim catered to. One of the Prophet's first companions, Abu Dharr al-Ghafari, railed at the new rulers: "This gold and silver of yours shall one day be heated red-hot in the fire of hell; and therewith shall you be seared on your foreheads, sides and backs, you ungodly spendthrifts."

Abu Dharr's carping was irritating. One of Uthman's appointees, Muawiya, decided to tempt Abu Dharr by sending him a purse full of gold coins—testing whether he could be corrupted by money. Within a few days, Muawiya asked for the coins back, claiming that he had made a mistake. The money was gone, however. Abu Dharr had already distributed it to the poor.

Abu Dharr wouldn't be silenced. He condemned Uthman's appointees: "You have departed from the ways of the Holy Prophet. You are amassing wealth, you have raised your palatial buildings and have become the victims of luxury!" Abu Dharr even upbraided Uthman himself. As punishment, Uthman had Abu Dharr banished to a desert outside Medina. Abu Dharr died two years later, a symbol of resistance against Uthman's corruption.

The general discontent with Uthman broke into open rebellion in 656. Muslim groups from various parts of the empire marched on Medina. Uthman, shocked by this resistance, promised to hear and address their complaints. The groups were satisfied and decided to return home. But as a group from Egypt traveled back to Alexandria, they captured a slave carrying a letter from Uthman. It was intended for the governor of Egypt. The letter told the governor to put the rebel leaders to death once they arrived in Alexandria.

Incensed by this treachery, the groups marched again on Medina. They confronted Uthman, who denied he had ever written the letter (historians are still unsure who wrote it). Uthman would not resign, but he would also not call on the empire to fight the rebels, since he would not sanction Muslim fighting Muslim. The situation settled into a tense and bitter standoff. When Uthman tried to give a sermon in a mosque, rebels threw stones at him, knocking him unconscious. Uthman's supporters carried him to his house, which the rebels insisted he could not leave.

In the following days, the rebels learned that a force loyal to Uthman was approaching. If they did not act, the rebels would be trapped. They attacked Uthman's barricaded house, finally overwhelming the spirited defenders. Realizing that his cause was hopeless, Uthman ordered his remaining servants and bodyguards to flee. Unprotected and alone, Uthman read calmly from his Quran as rebels broke into his bedroom. They stabbed him to death. The next day, the companions proclaimed Ali to be the new caliph.

THE "RIGHTLY GUIDED ONES"

The first four caliphs are remembered as the Rashidun, or "rightly guided ones." Each of them personally knew Muhammad and attempted to model his rule after the Prophet's example. Many Muslims remember their reigns as a golden era of Islam. The truth was more complicated, as three of the four first caliphs died from violent acts. Nonetheless, they are remembered as leaders who lived in relative simplicity in the small city of Medina and who knew the Prophet personally. They took part in the day-to-day affairs of their society and were close to the people.

This Italian illustration from the 1800s shows the first four caliphs, Abu Bakr, Umar, Uthman, and Ali.

CHAPTER SEVEN
EXPANSION AND TURMOIL

My fellow Christians delight in the poems and romances
of the Arabs. They study the works of Muhammadan
theologians and philosophers, not to refute them, but to
acquire a correct and elegant Arabic style. Alas!

—*Pablo Alvaro, bishop of Cordova, Spain, 854*

Ali, at last, was the caliph. His reign would be tragic,
however. His appointment was seen as a threat to those
who believed that no single person should control both the
political and the religious aspects of the Muslim Empire.
Unlike the first three caliphs, Ali intended to rule on
religious as well as political questions.

Ali also had powerful and embittered enemies. The
Prophet's widow, Aisha, had never forgiven Ali over the

affair of the necklace. Traveling from Mecca to Medina when she heard of Ali's appointment, she ordered the caravan to return to Mecca. Two of Ali's closest rivals, Zubayr and Talha, slipped out of Medina and joined her in Mecca. They later marched with a force to Basra, where they attempted to rally an army to support their quest for the caliphate.

Ali gathered an army and confronted Aisha, Zubayr, and Talha in the desert between Basra, Medina, and Mecca. Aisha entered the battle in a litter (passenger compartment) strapped to a large camel. The camel became a focal point in the combat as her followers rallied around her. In fierce

Aisha (in her litter) and Talha ride to Basra. The painting comes from an undated Persian manuscript.

fighting, Zubayr and Talha were killed, and Aisha's army scattered. Aisha, concealed inside the litter, by then bristling with spent arrows, was captured. Thus the Battle of the Camel ended. Ali pardoned Aisha and allowed her to return to Mecca.

After facing down this challenge, Ali began to remove the corrupt and ineffectual Uthman kinsmen who had held positions of power in the empire. Ali was determined to return Islam to what he believed the Prophet wanted—a simple, more reverent lifestyle. He emptied Uthman's treasury, distributing the funds to the needy and the poor.

Ali soon faced another challenge to his rule—a threat more serious than the one represented by Aisha. Uthman's appointee Muawiya ruled in Syria. He was related to Uthman and believed that his connection gave him the right to be caliph. His court in the city of Damascus was luxurious, a direct contradiction to Ali's vision of a more frugal Islam. Muawiya rallied a group of tribes to raise an army and avenge Uthman's murder. He displayed Uthman's shirt, bloody and full of holes from knife thrusts, in the mosque in Damascus.

In Medina, where most of the surviving companions still lived, Ali was advised to attack Muawiya and crush him. Muawiya, in the meantime, was also preparing for war. To free up his troops, he made a truce with the Byzantine emperor on his northern frontier.

Muawiya and Ali each marched at the head of their armies, confronting each other in western Persia at what became known as the Battle of Siffin. For days, champions from each side rode out to fight in individual combat.

Ali (top right) *leads his soldiers against Muawiya's army at the Battle of Siffin. The painting, which was made around 1825 by a Persian artist, illustrates a biography of Ali.*

The soldiers—Muawiya's wearing yellow cloths over their shoulders, Ali's wearing white—watched. Finally, the two armies drew closer and met in battle. After two days of combat, Ali's forces appeared to gain the upper hand.

At this crucial moment, according to legend, Muawiya's forces raised copies of the Quran on their spears. This gesture brought the fighting to a halt. It reminded the Muslims that they were fighting other Muslims, which the Quran strictly prohibits. The act also implied that the fight could be settled through arbitration—in which a judge would rule on a settlement. According to some stories, Ali accepted the pause in battle because Muhammad had insisted that Muslims should show mercy if their enemy asked for quarter. In other stories, the exhausted soldiers of both armies began to call for arbitration, bringing the battle to an abrupt halt. Ali, who was on the verge of victory, urged his soldiers to keep fighting, but they had lost their momentum.

While the exact details of the battle remain unclear, the result was not. Ali would never recover from this situation. After Ali agreed to arbitration, one part of his army, the Kharijites, abandoned him in rage and disgust. To them, Ali's decision to halt the fighting was an act of treachery akin to Muawiya's rebellion.

While the drawn-out arbitration took place, Ali had to deal with the Kharijites, who had withdrawn from the Arabian Peninsula altogether and settled near modern-day Baghdad, Iraq. Reluctantly, Ali ordered his army to march to the Kharijite encampment and subdue them by force.

While Ali was distracted in his dealings with the Kharijites, Muawiya had not been inactive. He had raised another army, which marched south from Syria and conquered the Holy Land (the areas surrounding Jerusalem) and Egypt. From Jerusalem, Muawiya proclaimed himself the new caliph.

Ali's rule was proving unpopular. Many Muslims had grown used to luxury and large stipends from the Muslim state. Ali's strident purity alienated potential allies.

Three Kharijites, disgusted at how Islam had been sullied in their eyes, plotted to simultaneously kill Muawiya, the general Amr, and Ali. The three Kharjirites split up, traveling to the cities where Muawiya, Amr, and Ali would publicly lead Friday prayers on a special holiday. One assassin approached Muawiya, but a guard

A 1307 Persian portrait of Ali carrying a two-bladed sword

spotted and subdued him. The assassin assigned to kill Amr mistakenly cut down the wrong man, not realizing that Amr had not attended the mosque that day. The third assassin, however, found Ali. Screaming, "Judgment belongs to God,

Ali, not to you!" he struck Ali in the head with a sword. The wound was shallow, but the blade had been coated with poison. Ali died two days later.

The death of Ali marked an ending to Islam's first age—and many Islamic historians see Ali's death as an end of innocence. Later, Muslim historians would remember the first four caliphs as "the rightly guided ones" who ruled during a golden era of Islam.

THE PRICE OF EMPIRE

Muawiya became the new caliph and moved the capital of the Islamic empire to Damascus. He ultimately was an effective caliph. He avoided religious controversy, leaving religious questions to scholars. But he secured his religious legitimacy by purchasing the right to oversee the Kaaba.

He centralized power through a strong army and navy. He promised his Arab soldiers that the empire's borders would continue to expand, with raids and longer campaigns using their energy—not civil war. Under Muawiya's direction, the Arab Muslims again turned their attention outward.

Muawiya appointed his son Yazid to succeed him. This choice may seem obvious, since virtually all emperors passed on their thrones to their offspring. Many Muslims, however, opposed the decision. They believed that Islam was a community—not an empire.

Muawiya died in 680, leaving his throne to his son as planned. A rebellion against Yazid brewed and exploded in Kufa. The rebels, believing that only a member of Muhammad's family could restore the Islamic community, looked to Ali's son Husayn to lead them. Husayn was skeptical of the Kufans' commitment to him, but he believed it was his duty to resist Yazid.

MASSACRE AT KARBALA

Yazid was well aware that Husayn wanted vengeance on the family that had supplanted Ali as caliph. Yazid ordered Husayn to appear before his governor in Medina and swear allegiance to his rule. Husayn appeared before the governor but—stalling for time—he asked to take the oath in public, where it would be more effective. The governor, impressed, agreed to Husayn's request. However, Husayn had no intention of giving the oath. He slipped out of Medina with his family and closest supporters and traveled toward Kufa to lead the rebellion.

When Yazid heard of Husayn's flight, he sent a Syrian army to Kufa. The army arrived before Husayn and crushed all resistance, executing the leaders of the rebellion. Husayn, still making his way toward the city, was walking into a trap. There was no way his group of less than one hundred could challenge an army of thousands.

Husayn soon learned of the events at Kufa. Nonetheless, he continued his march toward what was by then certain death. The Syrian army surrounded Husayn and his band at a place called Karbala. To thwart the Syrian cavalry, Husayn dug a trench around three sides of his camp (the fourth side was protected by hills), filled it with wood, and set it aflame. At the small entrance to the camp, he had his men kneel together with their lances pointing outward.

After failing to overwhelm the tiny band, the Syrian

soldiers decided to block Husayn's access to the nearby Euphrates River. When that was accomplished, all the soldiers had to do was wait. Slowly and painfully, Husayn's companions started dying from lack of water. His two sons and nephew were among the dead.

During the siege at Karbala, Husayn's half brother Abbas (lower right) fights his way back from a mission to get water from the Euphrates River. The painting comes from a Turkish book from the 1600s.

On the tenth day of the siege, Husayn staggered out of his tent, dizzy from thirst and in pain from wounds he had received earlier in the fighting. Using his last reserves of energy, he mounted a horse and charged the Syrian lines. The Syrian soldiers surrounded the lone rider and knocked him from his horse. The Syrian general dismounted and walked up to Husayn, by then barely alive. With a stroke of his sword, he severed Husayn's head from his body. The general ordered the head to be mounted on a lance and returned to Damascus, where it would be presented to Yazid on a gold platter. The Syrian soldiers finished their work by cutting down the remaining members of Husayn's band.

MOURNING HUSAYN'S DEATH

Husayn's rebellion was over, but the horror of the event reverberates to this day. The direct descendants of Muhammad had been savagely murdered by other Muslims. News of the massacre set off revolts throughout the Muslim Empire. Yazid's response was brutal. His armies trapped rebels and launched fireballs into both Mecca and Medina. Both cities were laid waste. The Kaaba was burned to the ground.

Although Yazid was able to smash the rebellions, Husayn's death was not forgotten. On the fourth anniversary of the massacre at Karbala, some residents from Kufa made a pilgrimage to Mecca. They had torn their shirts and dirtied their faces in acts of atonement because they had not supported Husayn. The residents returned the next year, and the year after that. They attracted followers who had supported Ali and his attempt to unite the caliphate and religious authority into the family of Muhammad. Ultimately, this group created a new branch of Islam—Shiite Islam. The name comes from the term *shi'at Ali*, or "followers of Ali."

THE SHIITE IMAMS

The Shiites long refused to acknowledge the first three caliphs. Instead, they consider Ali *(left)* to be the first imam—or spiritual leader of Islam. They consider Ali's two sons, Hasan *(center)* and Husayn *(right),* to be the second and third imams. Male descendents of Husayn (those who were not killed at Karbala) make up a line of imams that descended through the generations. The final imam, the twelfth, was born in 868. According to the Shiites, he was then hidden by God and will someday reappear to bring justice to the world.

With Husayn's death and the crushing of all subsequent resistance, Islam fell under the sway of the Umayyad dynasty. The Umayyads used Damascus as their capital city. But the original Muslim community, which had consisted of the companions with Muhammad in Medina, became the Muslim ideal, an example future generations of Muslims strived to follow.

CONQUERING THE WORLD

In 674 a Muslim army, supplied by the sea, landed outside the Byzantine capital of Constantinople. The Muslim troops were not able to break through the city's towering walls, but the siege lasted almost a decade. Constantinople barely survived.

By 680 Muslim forces had spread across North Africa. They reached the Atlantic Ocean and the tip of land across from Spain, from where they could glimpse the hills of the Spanish countryside rising out of the sea. Most of these soldiers were not Arabs but Berbers from North Africa who had recently converted to Islam. The army was led by an Arab general, Tariq ibn Ziyad, and was probably no larger than a few thousand men.

A German artist drew this portrait of Tariq ibn Ziyad in 1847.

Spain at that time was dominated by a Christian kingdom called Hispania. Its capital city was Toledo. The kingdom had lasted for centuries, but it had recently been thrown into confusion when a nobleman, Rodrigo, had seized the throne. The act left the kingdom politically weakened in the face of the Muslim threat. According to a legend, for generations a room in the king's palace had been locked shut. Each Spanish king added another padlock to the door when he took the throne. No one entered the sealed room. When Rodrigo proclaimed himself king, however, he demanded that the door be broken open. Inside, he found pictures of Arabs on the walls and an inscription that said that Spain would fall to the Muslims when the room was opened.

In 711 Tariq concealed his troops in common merchant ships to ferry them in groups to Spain's southern coast. After this force landed safely and established a beachhead, another five thousand soldiers arrived as reinforcements. Tariq ordered them to march north. It is possible that Tariq and his men received some aid from Spaniards. These supporters could have included Jews, who were severely persecuted in Hispania, as well as other citizens who were discontented with Rodrigo's rule. The Spaniards probably saw the Muslims as little more than raiders who would be gone by the end of the summer. As it turned out, the Muslims would remain in Spain for seven hundred years.

Tariq's forces met Rodrigo's in battle near the Guadelete River in southern Spain. There are no descriptions of the battle except a statement that Rodrigo's army was divided because of rivalry for the kingship. In any case, the Muslims killed Rodrigo and destroyed his army.

Tariq's army then moved swiftly. It subdued the city of Cordova after a three-month siege and conquered Toledo, the capital. When news of Tariq's victories spread to North Africa, the Muslim governor decided to raise an army of his own and also invade Spain. This force, numbering more than fifteen thousand, landed in 712. By 718 these two forces had conquered most of the Spanish peninsula.

This Spanish painting from around 1370 shows Spanish forces clashing with Muslims from northern Africa.

ARABS IN SPAIN

In Spain, Muslims created one of the most sophisticated societies in Europe. Arab philosophers helped reintroduce ancient Greek texts, which had been lost to western Europe after the fall of Rome. Muslim rulers established schools of higher learning in Spain's major cities. Students learned advanced mathematics and Greek philosophy. Jews, who had been persecuted under the previous Roman Catholic authorities, flourished in Muslim-controlled Spain. Throughout this period, the Catholic Church kept up an underground resistance. But Arab norms and culture dominated the country.

"My fellow Christians delight in the poems and romances of the Arabs," wrote one Christian bishop bitterly. "They study the works of Muhammadan theologians and philosophers, not to refute them, but to acquire a correct and elegant Arabic style. Alas! The young Christians who are most conspicuous for their talents have no knowledge of any literature save Arabic: they read and study avidly Arabic books."

Gradually, however, Spanish kings and the Catholic Church took back their country from the Muslims. In 1085 Toledo fell to Spanish forces. In 1236 the Spanish reconquered Cordova and forced the remaining Muslim state to pay tribute. In 1492 the last Muslim ruler in Spain surrendered to King Ferdinand and Queen Isabella.

THE TIDE IN EUROPE CRESTS AT POITIERS

Within a few years, Muslim raiders were crossing the spine of mountains that separate Spain from the rest of the European continent. In 732 a Muslim army marched into the land of the Franks (modern-day France). The size of the Muslim force may have been considerable—twenty or thirty thousand men on horses. They probed north, sacking towns for booty. Eventually, a Frankish army commanded by Charles Martel confronted the Muslim force.

Martel ordered his foot soldiers to form a line that stretched across a valley floor. Ridges on both sides of the Frankish position forced the Muslims to attack from the front. The Frankish soldiers were heavily armored and carried shields and spears, which they used to form a wall of metal. Martel and his soldiers were experienced and disciplined. When the Muslim cavalry charged, they held their position, stabbing and slashing at the horsemen as they rode past. "As a mass of ice, they stood firm together," wrote a chronicler at the time. The Muslim cavalry attacked the Franks for an entire day but were unable to penetrate Martel's line.

Both armies withdrew after the fighting, but the Franks were surprised to find the Muslim camp abandoned the next morning. The Muslim general was found dead on the battlefield, along with thousands of his soldiers. The Muslims' tents, filled with plunder, were also left behind.

The Battle of Poitiers, as it was called, is often depicted in the West as a turning point in history. Historians still disagree over its significance. Many argue that

Muslim writers at the time made little note of the battle, mentioning it only as the defeat of a minor raiding party. Others believe that it changed European history. After the battle, Muslim raiding parties and armies mostly confined themselves to Spain and did not venture farther into western Europe.

Charles Martel (center back) *fights with his soldiers against Muslim invaders in 732. This painting appears in a history of France completed in 1461.*

ARABIC ASCENDS

Before the Muslim conquests, Arabic was spoken only by desert tribes. After the conquests, it became a dominant world language. At first, Arab rulers allowed conquered peoples to use their previous language for official correspondence—Greek in the Byzantine world and Pahlavi in Persia. But in about 700, the caliph decreed that all government officials had to use Arabic in their records and correspondence. Suddenly, any person who had ambition to work in the government, regardless of background, had to know Arabic. As Islamic civilization flowered in the following centuries, Arabic became a universal language of science and philosophy.

RULERS OF THE WORLD

By 750 much of the Mediterranean and Middle Eastern world was part of the Muslim Empire. Some of these regions had been under Muslim rule for several generations. The local populations were gradually becoming Islamic. The empire enjoyed a new confidence and level of sophistication, wealth, and civilization.

A fascinating record of Muslim life around this time is provided by a Chinese soldier, Tu Huan, who had been captured in a battle with Muslim forces on the far eastern border of the empire. After ten years in Iraq, he was allowed to return home in 762. He compiled a chronicle of his time among the Muslims.

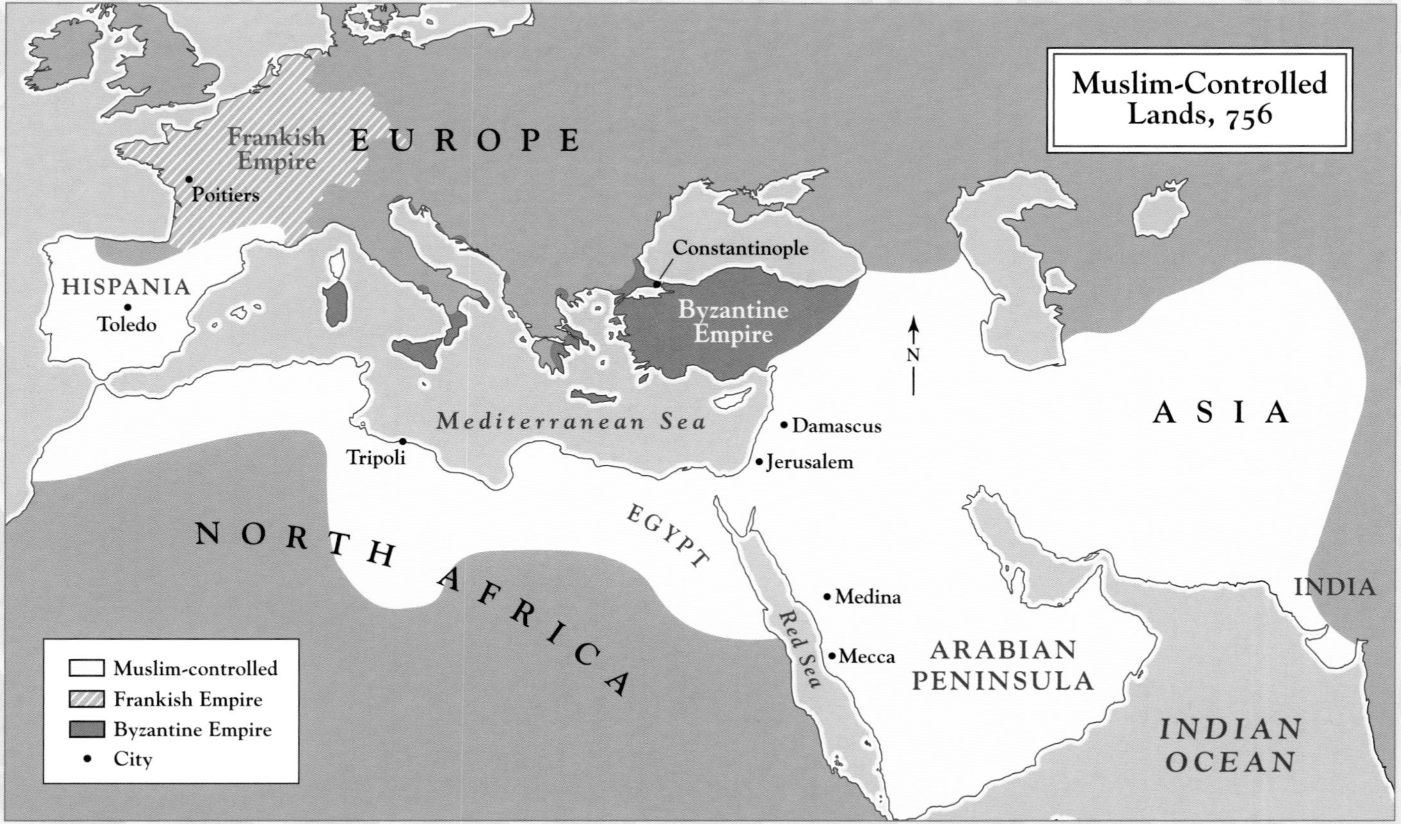

Map legend

- Muslim-controlled
- Frankish Empire
- Byzantine Empire
- • City

NORTH AFRICA

HISPANIA

Toledo

Poitiers

Frankish Empire

EUROPE

Tripoli

Mediterranean Sea

EGYPT

Red Sea

Byzantine Empire

Constantinople

Jerusalem

Damascus

Mecca

Medina

ARABIAN PENINSULA

N →

ASIA

INDIA

INDIAN OCEAN

Muslim-Controlled Lands, 756

"Both men and women are handsome and tall, and their manners are elegant," he wrote. "When a woman goes out in public, she must cover her face irrespective of her lofty or lowly social position. They perform ritual prayers five times a day." The Muslims "prohibit the drinking of wine and forbid music. When people squabble among themselves, they do not come to blows."

Tu Huan described a mosque that could hold thousands of people. In the mosque, he reported, the imam (prayer leader) delivered a sermon:

> Human life is very difficult, the path of righteousness is not easy, and adultery [cheating on a spouse] is wrong. To rob or steal, in the slightest way to deceive people with words, to make oneself secure by endangering others, to cheat the poor or oppress the lowly—there is no greater sin than one of these. All who are killed in battle against the enemies of Islam will achieve paradise. Kill the enemies, and you will receive happiness beyond measure.

Tu Huan's description reveals a people of refined dress and civilized manners—far different from their rugged ancestors who had established an empire. By then Muawiya's dynasty—the Umayyads—had fallen. After their collapse, the Muslim Empire broke up into smaller groups, each led by rival leaders. The caliphate still existed, but it was no longer a position that exercised full power. It no longer united Muslims under one ruler.

The Muslim heartlands—modern-day Saudi Arabia, Iraq,

Iran, and Afghanistan—experienced a series of invasions over the next several centuries. The conquerors came from central Asia. In each case, the new rulers adopted Islam. The frontiers of Islam continued to expand—beyond India and farther into Africa.

ISLAM AND SCIENCE

The extent of the Muslim conquests gave Arab Muslims exposure to a broad range of cultures. Muslim scientists and mathematicians were able to draw on a number of different sources—Greek, Indian, and Persian. Muslim mathematicians were especially innovative. They made lasting contributions to the study of algebra (the word *algebra* comes from the Arabic *al-jabr*, which means "joining of broken parts"). In astronomy, Muslim scientists *(below)* cast great doubt on the Greek-developed model that the other planets revolve around Earth. This critique was eventually translated into European languages and read by the European astronomer Copernicus. He ultimately declared that the planets revolve around the Sun, not Earth.

LOSING GROUND

In its dealings with Europe, Islam experienced reverses as well as gains. In the late 1090s, European knights called Crusaders invaded the Middle East. They wanted to retake Jerusalem and the Holy Land for Christianity. Bloody wars raged for nearly two centuries until Muslims were able to expel the Europeans. In 1453 Turkish Muslims seized Constantinople, finally destroying the last of the Byzantine Empire and creating the Ottoman Empire. In a rare defeat for Islam, Spanish Catholics overthrew the last Muslim rulers in Spain in 1492.

Crusaders capture Jerusalem in 1099 after a monthlong siege. European forces held the city for more than eighty-five years. A French artist created this painting in the late 1200s.

Starting in the 1700s, Muslim societies in the Middle East faced a changed Europe—one with sophisticated weapons, advanced science, and an aggressive spirit. In 1798 the French general Napoleon Bonaparte led an army into Egypt, which it quickly conquered (later, the British took control in Egypt). Over the next 150 years, European nations competed with each other to gain control of world territories. In this process, called colonialism, more and more Muslim nations fell under European rule.

With the end of World War I (1914–1918), the last Muslim empire—the Ottoman Empire, based in Turkey—disintegrated. With its collapse, European powers took control of lands that had been part of the first Muslim conquests. Great Britain took over Iraq and southern Iran. The French took Syria. Russia held power in northern Iran. In the Middle East, only Saudi Arabia, Turkey, and central Iran remained independent. The position of caliph, which had stretched back to Abu Bakr, officially ended in 1924.

In the twentieth century, European rule brought radical and wrenching changes for Muslims. European rulers tried to make the Middle East more like Europe. They built new schools, with new books and new kinds of lessons. They changed laws. They tried to wipe out old customs and ways of living that Europeans viewed as backward and out of touch with the modern world. In Iran, for instance, the European-backed leader ordered women to stop wearing veils—an old Islamic custom. When Iranian soldiers saw a woman wearing a veil, they grabbed it from her and ripped it to shreds with their bayonets.

Abdul Majid II (at throne) was the last caliph of the Ottoman Empire. The Turkish national assembly abolished the caliphate in 1922 and deposed Abdul Majid in 1924. This picture accompanies a 1924 French newspaper article announcing his exile.

Such changes left typical Muslims bewildered, confused, and angered. Under European control, a small number of rich Muslims prospered, while most people remained very poor. Frustrated, many Muslims sought a deeper connection to Islam. They saw in Islam's first hundred years an ideal—a time when a small community of believers, living under Muhammad, had created a community of God on earth.

THE HOPE AND CHALLENGE OF ISLAM

How could naked men, riding without armor or shield, have been able to win? Only a short period passed before the entire world was handed over to the Arabs; they subdued all fortified cities, taking control from sea to sea, and from east to west.

—*Jon Bar Penkaye, Christian monk and historian, 680s*

In 680 a Christian monk named Jon Bar Penkaye wrote a history of the world. The monk lived in a monastery in a corner of the Byzantine Empire—what in modern times is southeastern Turkey. There was much for the monk to write about, as the world had changed dramatically in fifty years. The Byzantine possessions in the Middle East had been shorn from the empire; the Persian Empire had been overwhelmed and destroyed.

"How could naked men, riding without armor or shield, have been able to win?" the monk wrote. "Only a short period passed before the entire world was handed over to the Arabs; they subdued all fortified cities, taking control from sea to sea, and from east to west." Jon Bar concluded: "'Their hand was upon everyone,' as the prophet says."

The Arab Muslim conquests are one of the great military feats in history. Within one hundred years of Muhammad's death, Arab Muslim armies had defeated two major empires. As Muslim armies entered the frontiers of India, another Arab army threatened the heart of France thousands of miles away. How did the Arab armies achieve such astonishing victories in so short a time?

Arab forces besiege the Byzantine city of Messina, located in modern-day Sicily, in 843. The painting comes from a thirteenth-century Sicilian copy of the Scylitzes Chronicle, which was written in the 1100s.

Like John Bar centuries ago, modern historians have no single answer. Some argue that the Arabs rose at a moment when the Byzantine and Persian empires were exhausted by war and the Mediterranean Basin had been devastated by plague, leaving the region relatively weak. If Muhammad had been born fifty years earlier, the Arabs may well have failed in their attempts to establish an empire.

Another theory is based on the supposedly rebellious state of the various Middle Eastern Christian communities at the time. Some Christian groups had suffered severe persecution under the Byzantines. Although there is no firm evidence, historians think that that discontent might have led some Christians to support the Arab Muslim armies, especially in Egypt. Christian Arabs who felt sympathetic to fellow Arabs, in Syria for example, might also have aided the Muslim armies.

In addition, Arab Muslim soldiers were tough, seasoned warriors, unified by Islam and passionate in their faith. Using their mobility and speed, they overcame opponent armies. The Muslim conquerors were able to hold on to their new territories, in part because they were fairly generous to the people they conquered. As long as subject people paid their taxes, the Muslims generally respected their property and their religion.

Whatever the reasons for the Muslim success—and perhaps it's a combination of all the factors listed above—the movements of the Arab armies in the first century of Islam broke the established order and created a new one in its place. Many territories that are strongly identified with Islam in modern times—for example, Syria, Egypt, Iraq, and Iran—were completely different cultures in preconquest times. Their elites spoke no Arabic, did not practice Islam, and looked to Constantinople and Rome for leadership and commerce. Within a few generations after the conquests, these areas were dominated by Arabic speakers. Their inhabitants had converted to Islam. They looked for inspiration to Mecca and Medina.

A RELIGION OF THE SWORD?

The success of the Arab conquests have led many to argue that Islam is a "religion of the sword," spread through the advance of armies. As early as the 630s, a Christian tract from Jerusalem captured this attitude. In a written dialogue, a Jewish man asks an elderly Christian wise man about the Prophet—Muhammad—who has appeared among the Arabs. "He is an imposter," the wise man replies. "Do the prophets come with sword and chariot?"

These words would echo repeatedly down the centuries, spoken usually by Christian Westerners—Europeans and Americans. When Muslims and Christians were active enemies—such as during the Crusades or when Muslim empires threatened European borders—it benefited the European cause to paint Islam as a violent religion.

The notion of early Islam spread by violence still lives in the twenty-first century. Roger Scruton, an English philosopher, wrote in 2002, "When Islam first spread across the Middle East and the southern Mediterranean, it was not by preaching and conversion in the Christian manner, but by conquest. The conquered people were given a choice: believe or die."

Many people disagree with this view. They point out that during Muhammad's time, religion and loyalty to one's state

ISLAM AND TERROR

In modern times, Western stereotypes of Islam as a "religion of the sword" have arisen again. Since the 1970s, images of Muslims acting violently have regularly appeared on television sets and in newspapers. Events such as suicide bombings, the Iranian Revolution (1979), and the 9/11 attacks have involved screaming Islamic crowds, hostage taking, and murderous acts of terrorism against innocent civilians. "Today, the traditional image of the Muslim horde has been more or less replaced by a new image: the Islamic terrorist, strapped with explosives, ready to be martyred for Allah, eager to take as many innocent people as possible with him," writes religious scholar Reza Aslan.

But Aslan argues that acts of terrorism and violence do not accurately represent Islam. He notes that the Muslim community widely condemns terrorism and views it as a violation of the Quran.

were the same thing. An empire (and its religion) did not survive, or expand, except through force. In this framework, early Islam was no more violent than the Christianity of the Byzantines or the Zoroastrianism of the Persians. In addition, rather than engaging in mindless violence, the first Arab armies followed rules of war. Arab leaders urged their soldiers to avoid needless destruction and the slaughter of civilians. The Arabs did not force Jews and Christians to convert to Islam. In contrast, the Byzantine and Persian armies were rarely as restrained or tolerant in their treatment of conquered peoples.

Historian Karen Armstrong believes that the religion of Islam can be separated from the first Arab conquests. "When the Arabs burst out of Arabia, they were not impelled by the ferocious power of Islam," Armstrong explains. "There was nothing religious about these campaigns, and Umar did not believe that he had a divine mandate [God's permission] to conquer the world." Umar, according to Armstrong, was not driven by religion but instead wanted plunder and an activity to keep the Muslim community unified.

THE FUTURE AND THE PAST

The results of the Arab conquests are clear in our modern world. In the twenty-first century, more than one billion people practice Islam. Although based in the Middle East, the religion has spread worldwide—from Southeast Asia to Africa to the Americas.

For Muslims, religion infuses daily life in hundreds of small ways, through rituals, customs, and habits. For instance, Islam requires people to pray five times a day and urges them to make a pilgrimage to Mecca at least once in a lifetime. During the holy month of Ramadan, Muslims fast each day from sunrise to sunset. These practices are not just in people's heads but in their hearts.

To understand the Islamic people we must understand the power of Islam—a faith that stretches back more than fourteen hundred years. That understanding must begin with Islam's first century—when the Arabs suddenly and irrevocably altered the world.

PRIMARY SOURCE RESEARCH

To learn about historical events, people study many sources, such as books, websites, newspaper articles, photographs, and paintings. These sources can be separated into two general categories—primary sources and secondary sources.

A primary source is the record of an eyewitness or someone who lived around the time being studied. Primary sources often provide firsthand accounts about a person or event. Examples include diaries, letters, autobiographies, speeches, newspapers, and oral history interviews. Libraries, archives, historical societies, and museums often have primary sources available on-site or on the Internet.

A secondary source is published information that was researched, collected, and written or otherwise created after the event in question. Authors and artists who create secondary sources use primary sources and other secondary sources in their research, but they interpret and arrange the source material in their own works. Secondary sources include history books, novels, biographies, movies, documentaries, and magazines. Libraries and museums are filled with secondary sources.

After finding primary and secondary sources, authors and historians must evaluate them. They may ask questions such as: Who created this document? What is this person's point of view? What biases might this person have? How trustworthy is this document? Just because a person was an eyewitness to an event does not mean that the person recorded the whole truth about that event. For example, a soldier describing a battle might depict only the heroic actions of his unit and only the brutal behavior of the enemy. An account from a soldier on the opposing side might portray the same battle very differently. When sources disagree, researchers must decide through additional study which explanation makes the most sense. For this reason, historians consult a variety of primary and secondary sources. Then they can draw their own conclusions.

The Pivotal Moments in History series takes readers on a journey to important junctures in history that shaped our modern world. Authors researched each event using both primary and secondary sources, an approach that enhances readers' awareness of the complexities of the materials and helps bring to life the rich stories from which we draw our understanding of our shared history.

RESEARCHING THE ARAB CONQUESTS

The early days of Islam present a fascinating puzzle to modern historians. At first glance, one finds an enormous number of primary sources, as well as secondary sources written shortly after Muhammad's death.

First, the Quran and the hadith contain a number of clues about Muhammad and Arabian society at the time of the founding of Islam. Many of these clues are vague, however. For example, one verse from the Quran describes "the opening" and people "joining the religion of God."

This fragment contains a letter supposedly written by Muhammad to a Persian shah (ruler), inviting the shah to convert to Islam. Scholars believe that the fragment may be a copy of the original letter from the early 600s.

Many scholars believe that this text refers to Muhammad's triumphant entry into Mecca. Other scholars disagree. They suggest that the verse was revealed earlier, when Muhammad was still in Medina. Scholars don't dispute that the verse describes an event that actually occurred—they just don't know which event. Thus, although the Quran and the hadith offer information that may be historically accurate, they don't always give specific details.

Another important early source is a biography of Muhammad compiled in the century after his death. The information comes from stories about the first days of Islam, told in the years after Muhammad's death. By this time, many of Muhammad's original companions had also died. The stories were already receding into memory and legend. In the mid-700s, a scholar, Muhammad al-Zuhri, began collecting the stories to compile them into a biography. Al-Zuhri died before he completed his project, but one of his assistants, Muhammad ibn Ishaq, carried on and finished his work. Ibn Ishaq methodically and relentlessly interviewed Medina residents about Muhammad. He cross-checked their testimony to weed out inconsistencies and distortions. Ibn Ishaq's biography remains the primary written source about Muhammad's life.

Other books about the early days of Islam followed. These works include *Conquests of the Lands* by al-Baladhuri, written in the ninth century, and *History of Prophets and Kings*, by al-Tabari, written in the tenth century.

The early Arab texts provide many problems for researchers. For one thing, many of them are contradictory and obscure. They often dwell on material that draws little of our interest in modern times—such as a list of generals of Arab armies, or speeches supposedly given on the eve of battle—and ignore details about military campaigns or dates that the modern historian craves.

The early works are also based on oral tradition—the passing down of stories, in spoken form, from one generation to the next. The oral tradition served many purposes in Muslim society. For instance, stories passed on to younger generations promoted values that were important to Muslims, such as honor, courage, and faith. But the stories were not always intended to be exact, fact-based accounts of historical events. What's more, the stories changed over time. Different storytellers altered details, characters, and the order of events, perhaps because they misremembered them or perhaps to make their own ancestors look more heroic.

Modern historians sifting through the early writings about Islam come up with only a few solid facts. These facts are the basis of most modern histories of the era—including this one. But writers must acknowledge that their texts can be, at best, only reasonable constructions of events, not accounts based on solid historical evidence. It simply doesn't exist.

PRIMARY SOURCE: SPEECH TO A PERSIAN SHAH

The primary sources about the Arab conquests have their own stories to tell. These may not reveal facts that modern readers would deem most important, but they reveal much about Arab attitudes in the early days of Islam. These narratives set out ideals and models of character that were important to Muslims. They reveal the worldview of the Arab armies.

One Arab account, written about 900, describes an Arab leader speaking to a Persian shah (ruler). The incident takes place in about 636. In the following passage, the speaker tells the shah how Muhammad changed Arab society:

> There was nobody more destitute than we were. As for hunger, it was not hunger in the usual sense. We used to eat beetles of various sorts, scorpions and snakes and we considered this our food. Nothing but the bare earth was our dwelling. We wore only what we spun from the hair of camels and sheep. Our religion was to kill one another and raid one another. There were those among us who would bury our daughters alive, not wanting them to eat our food. But then God sent us a well-known man. We knew his lineage, his face and his birthplace. His land is the best part of our land. His glory and the glory of his ancestors are famous among us. His family is the best of our families, and his tribe the best of our tribes. He himself was the best among

us and at the same time, the most truthful and the most forbearing. He invited us to embrace his religion. He spoke and we spoke; he spoke the truth and we lied. He grew in stature and we became smaller. Everything he said came to pass. God instilled in our hearts belief in him and caused us to follow him.

It is improbable that these words were ever spoken by one person in one place. The text can be considered a summary of views held in common by Arab Muslims. The first sentences describe a people with little civilization. They struggle on the verge of starvation, subsisting on insects and snakes. Their clothes are little more than rude garments. They kill one another thoughtlessly, without mercy or remorse. They bury infant daughters because sons were more highly valued, and an extra mouth in the desert strained food supplies.

Overall, this text should not be considered a literal depiction of Arab tribal life before Muhammad. However, the words reveal how Muslims considered the period before Muhammad to be a time of darkness, with little morality or culture. The snake and scorpion, eaten for food, have a double meaning—the snake is a symbol of evil, and the scorpion was dreaded for its savage sting. More important, the speaker condemns the pre-Islamic practice of killing and raiding other Arabs in a retaliatory fashion. Muhammad forbade Muslims to slay other Muslims.

The latter half of the statement addresses how Muhammad was at first not accepted by Meccan Arabs: "He spoke and we spoke; he spoke the truth and we lied. He grew in stature and we became smaller." The speaker shows how Muhammad was gradually accepted, his position growing over time while that of his opponents declined.

Other themes are also worth noting. The Arabs remember Muhammad for teaching them how to live a moral life, but they also suggest that, by following Allah's commands, they were rewarded: "Everything he said came to pass." In this language, we can see how Islam and its early worldly success were intertwined.

TIMELINE

c. 570   Muhammad is born in Mecca, Saudi Arabia.

c. 610   In a cave on Mount Hira, Muhammad receives his
             first message from Allah.

622   Muhammad and his followers settle in Yathrib, later
             called Medina. The event is later dated as the first
             year of the Muslim calendar.

624   Muhammad and his followers defeat the Quraysh at
             the Battle of Bedr.

Muhammad's forces (right) *meet the Quraysh at the 624 Battle of Bedr.*

627   Muhammad again defeats the Quraysh at the Battle
             of the Trench.

630   Muhammad captures Mecca and smashes the idols
             in the Kaaba.

632	Muhammad dies. Abu Bakr becomes the first caliph.
632–633	In the Ridda Wars, Abu Bakr crushes rebellions against his rule.
634	Persian forces defeat a Muslim army at the Battle of the Bridge. Abu Bakr dies. Umar becomes the second caliph.
635	Muslim armies conquer Damascus, Syria.
636	Muslim armies destroy the Byzantine army at the Battle of Yarmuk.
636, 637, OR 638	Muslim forces defeat the Persians at the Battle of Qadisiya.
638	Sophronius surrenders Jerusalem to Muslim forces.

In this illustration from the 1800s, Umar (standing center) enters Jerusalem on foot after the city's 638 surrender.

139

640 Muslim armies invade Egypt.

641 The Byzantine emperor Heraclius dies.

642 Amr occupies Alexandria, the capital of Egypt.

644 An assassin kills Umar. Uthman becomes the third caliph. Uthman's forces put down a rebellion in Alexandria.

CA. 650 Uthman orders the creation of a standard written version of the Quran.

Few copies of the Quran remain from the early years of Islam. This page once decorated the beginning of a Quran from the 700s.

656 An assassin kills Uthman. Ali becomes the fourth caliph. Ali fights off revolts in the Battle of the Camel.

657	The Battle of Siffin ends in a standoff between Ali and Muawiya.
661	A Kharijite assassin kills Ali. Muawiya proclaims himself caliph and moves the capital of the Islamic Empire to Damascus.
680	Muawiya dies. His son Yazid becomes caliph. Husayn leads a rebellion against Yazid's rule. Yazid's forces slaughter Husayn and his band at Karbala.

Husayn (center) *fights Yazid in this painting from the early 1900s depicting the Battle of Karbala in 680.*

711	Muslim armies begin their takeover of Spain.
732	Under Charles Martel, a Frankish army defeats Muslims at the Battle of Poitiers in France.

GLOSSARY

ALLAH: the Arabic name for God—the supreme being in the Islamic religion

CALIPHS: the successive leaders of Islam from the time of Muhammad's death until 1924

HADITH: a group of sayings and traditions concerning Muhammad and his companions

HEGIRA: Muhammad's journey to Medina in 622

IDOL: an image or symbol representing a god

MONOTHEISM: the doctrine or belief that there is only one god. Islam, Judaism, and Christianity are monotheistic religions.

MOSQUE: an Islamic house of worship

PILGRIM: someone who journeys to a holy place

POLYTHEISM: belief in or worship of more than one god

PROPHET: a person who reveals messages from God

QURAN: the Islamic holy book, consisting of Allah's messages to Muhammad

SHIITE: a member of one of the two major branches of Islam. Shiites believe that Ali was Muhammad's rightful successor and that Islamic leaders should be chosen from his descendants.

SIEGE: a military tactic in which an army surrounds a town or enemy base, cutting it off from food and supplies

SUNNI: a member of one of the two major branches of Islam. Sunnis believe that a group of religious scholars were the rightful successors to Muhammad and that anyone can be an Islamic leader.

SURA: a chapter of the Quran

TRIBUTE: a payment by one ruler or nation to another as a sign of submission or as the price of protection

WHO'S WHO?

ABU BAKR (c. 573–634) Abu Bakr became the caliph of

the Muslim community after Muhammad's death in 632. Although Bakr lived only two years more, he made crucial decisions that preserved Islam and prepared it for growth. Bakr was an elderly man when he became caliph over the objections of Ali and his supporters. He was considered gentle, kind, and full of wisdom. Under his direction, Muslims crushed all revolts against Islam immediately following Muhammad's death. Islam soon spread across the Arabian Peninsula. Realizing that Bedouin Islamic unity could not be sustained unless its energy was directed against outsiders, Bakr ordered the first invasions of the empires to the north, which ultimately resulted in spectacular victories. During his short but important reign, Abu Bakr solidified the new religion. Under his direction, Islamic power threatened the borders of the Byzantine Empire. In his last days, he prevented internal strife by ensuring Umar's smooth succession to power.

AISHA (614–678) Aisha was Abu Bakr's daughter and Muhammad's beloved wife. Sunnis believe that Muhammad died with his head cradled in her lap, although Shiites believe that he was with Ali when he died. Ali and Aisha were bitter enemies, according to legend, because of the Scandal of the Necklace. After Ali became caliph, Aisha helped organize a rival army that was defeated in the Battle of the Camel. Aisha was captured after the battle and did not contest for power again.

ALI (598–661) Ali was Muhammad's cousin, one of

his earliest converts, and one of his companions. After Muhammad's death, Ali and his supporters argued bitterly that the position of caliph should be his. Three times, however, Muhammad's other companions selected another candidate. They argued that the caliphate should not become a hereditary position. Ali finally became the fourth caliph. His reign was short and tragic. He faced rebellions from supporters and family members of the former caliph Uthman. After nearly defeating Muawiya in battle, Ali was effectively outmaneuvered in the following negotiations. Ali died shortly afterward, killed by an assassin who believed he had betrayed Islam.

AMR IBN AL-AS (?–663) Amr was one of the most successful generals of the first Arab Muslim conquests. After Muhammad's death, he was an important commander of the forces that conquered Syria. He then led an army into Egypt, where he successfully laid siege to Alexandria. Amr was later dismissed from his post by the caliph Uthman. Amr still commanded the loyalty of his soldiers and their families. More than a decade after his dismissal, he led an army into Egypt in support of Muawiya's rebellion against Uthman.

FATIMA (c. 616–633) Born in Mecca, Fatima was a

daughter of Muhammad and Khadija. She accompanied her father to Medina in 622. She married Ali and gave birth to two sons, Husan and Husayn, whose followers founded Shiite Islam. Fatima clashed with Abu Bakr, her husband's rival for the caliphate. She died one year after her father's death.

HERACLIUS (c. 575–641) Heraclius was the Byzantine

emperor when Muslim armies conquered Syria and Palestine. A fierce and resourceful military leader, Heraclius led the Byzantine Empire out of chaos during its war with the Persian Empire, leading a bold counterattack that resulted in Byzantine victory. Heraclius was not prepared for the Muslim onslaught that appeared out of Arabia. His army was destroyed at the Battle of Yarmuk, which led to the loss of vast amounts of Byzantine territory.

HUSAYN (626–680) Husayn was Ali and Fatima's son and Muhammad's grandson. After Ali's death, Husayn led a revolt against the caliph Yazid. At the city of Kufa, Yazid's forces massacred most of Husayn's followers. Husayn continued on to Karbala, where he and the rest of his band were killed. Husayn would later be celebrated as a martyr by the Shiites.

KHADIJA (?–619) Khadija was Muhammad's first wife. She had previously been married to a wealthy Meccan merchant. When he died, Khadija took over his business. She hired Muhammad to trade goods for her, and they soon married. Together they had six children, only four of whom lived to adulthood. Khadija was Muhammad's first convert to Islam. He did not take any other wives until after her death.

KHALID IBN AL-WALID (?–642) Khalid, one of the leading generals of the Arab conquests, earned the nickname Sword of God for his exploits. Khalid played a major role in the Ridda Wars and in the winning of Syria and Palestine from the Byzantines. Historical sources are unclear, but Khalid may have led the Muslim army at the Battle of Yarmuk, where the Byzantine army was destroyed.

MUAWIYA (c. 602–680) Muawiya was a member of the Meccan elite and a late convert to Islam. A supporter of Uthman, he challenged Ali after Uthman's death. After Ali's assassination, Muawiya proclaimed himself caliph and moved the base of power to Damascus, Syria. Muawiya designated his son Yazid the next caliph. This act angered many Muslims because it made the caliph a dynastic position (one passed down through a single family).

MUHAMMAD (c. 570–632) Muhammad founded Islam, one of the world's major religions, in the seventh century. Born in Mecca in about 570, Muhammad was orphaned at a young age. He was raised by his uncle and became a successful businessman. About the age of forty, Muhammad began to receive messages from Allah. These messages, later compiled in the Quran, became the basis of Islam. Muhammad clashed with the Meccan elite over the new religion, finally prevailing and converting the city about 630. Under Muhammad's direction, the faith spread through the Arab tribes on the Arabian Peninsula. Muhammad died around 632. He is revered for his courage, compassion, and wisdom. Muslims commonly refer to him simply as the Prophet.

UMAR (c. 586–644) Umar was the second caliph of the

Muslim community after Muhammad's death. Under Umar's rule, the Muslim army won astounding victories and established the basis for an empire. Umar was described as brusque, severe, disciplined, and honest. He humbled his greatest generals but patiently heard out villager quarrels over cows and other small matters. Frugal and industrious, he laid out the rules by which Arab soldiers were to live in separate garrison cities in the conquered territories. Even as the Muslims grew wealthy from tribute, he insisted that no man live in a home more extravagant than the Prophet's humble dwelling. Assassinated at the age of sixty-three, Umar is remembered as one of the great caliphs.

UTHMAN (?–656) Uthman was the third caliph of the

Muslim community after Muhammad's death. Uthman divided the community, awarding positions of power and prestige exclusively to members of his family and tribe. He ignored warnings of revolt until it was too late. Rebellious armies surrounded his home in Medina, forced their way in, and stabbed Uthman to death as he read the Quran. Uthman's most positive legacy is that he established the definitive edition of the Quran.

SOURCE NOTES

4 Reza Aslan, *No God but God: The Origins, Evolution and Future of Islam* (New York: Random House, 2005), 34.

5 Ibid.

5 Ibid., 38.

6 Ibid., 39.

44 Richard Fletcher, *The Cross and the Crescent* (London: Penguin Books, 2003), 9.

12 Hugh Kennedy, *The Great Arab Conquests* (Philadelphia: Perseus Books Group, 2007), 41.

18 Aslan, *No God but God*, 40.

18 Michael Sells, *Approaching the Quran* (Ashland, OR: White Cloud Press, 1999), 82.

28 Barnaby Rogerson, *The Heirs of Muhammad: Islam's First Century and the Origins of the Sunni-Shia Split* (Woodstock, NY: Overlook Press, 2006), 26.

30 Ibid., 54.

33 Kennedy, *Great Arab Conquests*, 51.

37 Aslan, *No God but God*, 121.

38 Ibid., 129.

39 Ibid., 40.

39 Ibid., 33.

40 Ibid., 134.

42 Ibid., 129.

43 Ibid., 132.

45 Rogerson, *Heirs of Muhammad*, 149.

46 David Nicolle, *Armies of the Muslim Conquest* (Oxford: Osprey Publishing, 1993), 8.

47 Kennedy, *Great Arab Conquests*, 41–42.

48 Ibid., 49.

52 Walter Kaegi, *Byzantium and the Early Islamic Conquests* (Cambridge: Cambridge University Press, 1992), 26.

56 Kennedy, *Great Arab Conquests*, 146.

58 Rogerson, *Heirs of Muhammad*, 179.

58 Aslan, *No God But God*, 122.

60 Kennedy, *Great Arab Conquests*, 83.

61 Ibid., 85.

62 Rogerson, *Heirs of Muhammad*, 179.

62 Kennedy, *Great Arab Conquests*, 50.

63 Francis Robinson, ed., *Cambridge Illustrated History of the Islamic World* (Cambridge: Cambridge University Press,

1996), 17.

63 Ibid., 226.

66 Rogerson, *Heirs of Muhammad*, 182.

71 Kennedy, *Great Arab Conquests*, 115.

73 Robinson, *History of the Islamic World*, 11.

74 Rogerson, *Heirs of Muhammad*, 214.

79 Ibid., 215.

80 Ibid.

81 Ibid., 217.

83 Robinson, *History of the Islamic World*, 25.

84 Rogerson, *Heirs of Muhammad*, 220.

85 Ibid., 223.

85 Ibid.

88 Ibid., 273.

90 Ibid., 240.

97 Rogerson, *Heirs of Muhammad*, 273.

97 Ibid.

100 Crane Brinton, *A History of Civilization* (New York: Prentice-Hall, Inc., 1955), 361.

105 Kennedy, *Great Arab Conquests*, 135.

114 Brinton, *A History of Civilization*, 361.

115 Victor Davis Hanson, *Carnage and Culture* (New York: Random House, 2001), 138.

119 Kennedy, *Great Arab Conquests*, 360–361.

124 Kennedy, *Great Arab Conquests*, 1.

125 Ibid.

127 Fletcher, *Cross and Crescent*, 16.

127 Roger Scruton, "Religion of Peace? Islam, Without the Comforting Clichés," *National Review* 24 (December 31, 2002), 43–46.

128 Aslan, *No God But God*, 79.

129 Karen Armstrong, *Islam: A Short History*, (New York: Random House, 2000). 87.

136 Abu Ja'far Muhammad Tabari, *The History of al-Tabari*, translated by Yohanan Friedmann (Albany: State University of New York, 1985), 37–38.

SELECTED BIBLIOGRAPHY

PRIMARY SOURCES

Ibn Ishaq. *The Life of Muhammad*. 700s. Reprint. Oxford: Oxford University Press, 2002.

John of Nikiu. *Chronicle of John, Bishop of Nikiu*. c. 690. Reprint. Merchantville, NJ: Evolution Publications, 2007.

Maurice's Strategikon: Handbook of Byzantine Military Strategy. 550–600. Reprint. Philadelphia: University of Pennsylvania Press, 1984.

Nicephorus, Patriarch of Constantinople. *Short History*. c. 800. Reprint. Washington, DC: Dumbarton Oaks, Research Library and Collection, 1990.

Penkaye, Jon Bar. "Ris Melle." 650–700. Reprint. *Jerusalem Studies in Arabic and Islam* 9 (1987), 51–75.

Tabari, Abu Ja'far Muhammad. *The History of al-Tabari*. Translated by Yohanan Friedman. c. 900. Reprint. Albany: State University of New York, 1985.

Yaqubi, Ahmad b. Abi Yaqub. *Tarikh*. 2 vols. Late 800s. Reprint. Leiden, Netherlands: Brill, 1883.

SECONDARY SOURCES

Armstrong, Karen. *Islam: A Short History*. New York: Random House, 2000.

Aslan, Reza. *No God but God: The Origins, Evolution, and Future of Islam*. New York: Random House, 2005.

Brinton, Crane. *A History of Civilization: Vol. 1*. New York: Prentice-Hall, Inc., 1955.

Fletcher, Richard. *The Cross and the Crescent: The Dramatic Story of the Earliest Encounters between Christians and Muslims*. London: Penguin Books, 2003.

Glubb, John Bagot. *The Great Arab Conquests*. London: Hodder and Stoughton, Ltd., 1963.

Hanson, Victor Davis. *Carnage and Culture: Landmark Battles in the Rise of Western Power.* New York: Random House, 2001.

Hodgson, Marshall. *The Venture of Islam: The Classical Age of Islam Vol. 1.* Chicago: University of Chicago Press, 1974.

Kaegi, Walter. *Byzantium and the Early Islamic Conquests.* Cambridge: Cambridge University Press, 1992.

Kennedy, Hugh. *The Great Arab Conquests.* Philadelphia: Perseus Books Group, 2007.

Lawrence, Bruce. *The Qur'an: A Biography.* New York: Atlantic Monthly Press, 2006.

Lewis, Bernard. *The Crisis of Islam: Holy War and Unholy Terror.* New York: Random House, 2002.

———. *From Babel to Dragomans: Interpreting the Middle East.* New York: Oxford University Press, 2004.

Naipaul, V. S. *Among the Believers: An Islamic Journey.* New York: Random House, 1981.

———. *Beyond Belief: Islamic Excursions Among the Converted Peoples.* New York: Random House, 1998.

Nicolle, David. *Armies of the Muslim Conquest.* Oxford: Osprey Publishing, 1993.

Robinson, Frances, ed. *Cambridge Illustrated History: Islamic World.* Cambridge: Cambridge University Press, 1996.

Rogerson, Barnaby. *The Heirs of Muhammad: Islam's First Century and the Origins of the Sunni-Shia Split.* Woodstock, NY: Overlook Press, 2006.

Sells, Michael. *Approaching the Quran: The Early Revelations.* Ashland, OR: White Cloud Press, 1999.

Stewart, Desmond. *Great Ages of Man: Early Islam.* New York: Time Life Books, 1967.

FURTHER READING AND WEBSITES

BOOKS

Broberg, Catherine. *Saudi Arabia in Pictures*. Minneapolis: Twenty-First Century Books, 2003.

Gordon, Matthew S. *Islam*. New York: Duncan Baird Publishers, 2002.

Hyde, Margaret O., and Emily G. Hyde. *World Religions 101: An Overview for Teens*. Minneapolis: Twenty-First Century Books, 2008.

January, Brendan. *The Iranian Revolution*. Minneapolis: Twenty-First Century Books, 2008.

Jones, Rob Lloyd. *The Story of Islam*. Tulsa, OK: EDC Publishing, 2007.

Kort, Michael G. *The Handbook of the Middle East*. Minneapolis: Twenty-First Century Books, 2008.

Marchant, Kerena. *Muhammad and Islam*. London: Hodder Wayland, 2005.

Nicolle, David. *Armies of the Muslim Conquest*. Oxford: Osprey Publishing, 1993.

Thompson, Jan. *Islam*. North Vancouver: Whitecap Books, 2004.

Time-Life Books. *What Life Was Like in the Lands of the Prophet: Islamic World, AD 570–1405*. Alexandria, VA: Time-Life Books, 1999.

VIDEOS

Inside Islam. New York: A&E Home Video, 2002. DVD.

Inside Mecca. Washington, DC: National Geographic Video, 2003. DVD.

Islam: Empire of Faith. Arlington, VA: PBS Paramount, 2005. DVD.

WEBSITES

BBC
  Religion and Ethics—Islam
  http://www.bbc.co.uk/religion/religions/islam/index.shtml
  This website from the British Broadcasting Corporation provides a solid background on Islam, its beliefs, its practices, and the

perspective of its followers. In addition, the site provides numerous links to news stories—both present and past—that involve Islam in some way.

PBS
Islam: Empire of Faith
http://www.pbs.org/empires/islam/
This site is the web accompaniment to the PBS video of the same name. It offers interactive features that allow visitors to explore Islam's history more closely.

Visual Geography Series
http://www.vgsbooks.com
Visitors to this site can find links to more information about the countries of the Middle East. Read about the land, history, government, people, culture, and economy of Egypt, Greece, Iran, Iraq, Israel, Jordan, Saudi Arabia, Spain, and many other countries influenced by the rise of Islam.

INDEX

ABOUT THE AUTHOR

Brendan January is an award-winning author of more than twenty nonfiction books for young readers, including *The Iranian Revolution, Genocide, Globalize It!, The Stories of the IMF, the World Bank, the WTO,* and *Those Who Protest.* Educated at Haverford College and Columbia Graduate School of Journalism, January was also a Fulbright Scholar in Germany. He lives with his wife and two children in Maplewood, New Jersey.

PHOTO ACKNOWLEDGMENTS